A YEAR IN CHEESE

A SEASONAL CHEESE COOKBOOK

ANDROUET

ARIS LONDON STOCKH

ASONAL CHE

SINCE 190

A YEAR IN CHEESE

A SEASONAL CHEESE COOKBOOK

ALEX AND LÉO GUARNERI
RECIPES BY ALESSANDRO GRANO

PHOTOGRAPHY BY KIM LIGHTBODY

F

FRANCES LINCOLN LIMITED

Frances Lincoln Limited
74–77 White Lion Street
London N1 9PF
www.franceslincoln.com

A Year in Cheese
Copyright © Frances Lincoln Limited 2015
Text © The Cheesemonger Ltd 2015
Photographs © Kim Lightbody 2015
Design: Glenn Howard
Commissioning editor: Zena Alkayat

First Frances Lincoln edition 2015

A catalogue record for this book is available from the British Library.

ISBN 978-0-7112-3641-7

Printed and bound in China

1 2 3 4 5 6 7 8 9

To our parents, our collaborators (both past and present) and all our producers

CONTENTS

18
Introduction
What is seasonal cheese?

22
Alex and Léo Guarneri
About the brothers

24
Androuet
Selling and maturing
seasonal cheese since 1909

26
A note on the recipes
Alessandro Grano

28
Spring
Goats' curd, Brillat-Savarin
and the fresh cheeses

66
Summer
Ricotta, Mozzarella
and the soft cheeses

100
Autumn
Cheddar, Gruyère and the
semi-hard cheeses

130
Winter
Reblochon, Comté and the
bold cheeses

174
Cheeseboards
The perfect selection

176
Complementary wines
Pairing wine with cheese

180
Index

186
Acknowledgements

INTRODUCTION

Left: The Comté maturing caves (*caves d'affinage*) at Fort des Rousses in Eastern France. Contents page: Tommette de Chèvre cheese. Introductory images: The regions of Savoie, Beaufort and the Midi-Pyrénées

There's something magical about cheese: its endless diversity, its unique flavours, its delicious transformations in recipes both savoury and sweet. We wanted this book to be a celebration of this most treasured dairy product, but in particular, a celebration of seasonal cheese.

Seasonal cheese is what we sell in our London fromagerie Androuet and it's what we serve right next door in our restaurant. Our seasonal ethos is something we share with our Androuet cousins in France. There are eight Androuet fromageries across the Channel, and the founding shop in Paris has been selling seasonal cheese since 1909.

Cheese can be used in cooking in so many ways with so many different results, so together with our Italian chef Alessandro Grano, we've collected our favourite recipes to share with you. There are some surprising combinations (like pork belly with Pecorino, or ice cream with Cornish Blue) as well as classic cheese dishes (raclette, fondue and the best croque-monsieur you'll ever eat).

We've used an incredible variety of interesting and tasty cheeses from artisan producers. But we've also included clear descriptions so you can find alternative cheeses in your local store. If you live near an artisan fromagerie and can source seasonal cheese, you'll find there's nothing better than cheese that's been made with the love, care and passion of an expert producer at the right time of year. But just find the best cheese you can and eat it when it's at its prime. We think you'll be converted.

Bon appétit!

Alex and Léo Guarneri

WHAT IS SEASONAL CHEESE?

We realise most people don't think of cheese as being seasonal, but it's really just like fruit, vegetables and meat: every cheese has a time of year when it reaches its best. Seasonal cheese is about listening to nature, understanding the grazing and birthing cycle of the animal that's being milked, knowing what they're eating at which time of year, and recognising optimal maturing and ageing times. Other conditions can affect cheese seasonality too, such as climate, the elevation of the farm and the region where the producer is situated.

There's always an ideal time to produce different cheeses so that they taste as good as possible. This approach is not new – it's a traditional practice that most of us somehow lost sight of. By returning to this and insisting on an awareness of seasonality, we are not only showing respect to the animals and the cheese, but also ensuring that the cheese is at its tastiest.

At the beginning of each chapter – Spring, Summer, Autumn and Winter – there's a brief breakdown of what's in season and why, plus a seasonal cheeseboard at the end of each chapter for you to try for yourself. We hope it inspires you to stick to the seasons and enjoy cheese more than ever!

ABOUT THE GUARNERI BROTHERS

We grew up loving food as young boys. Our grandfather was a food importer and our mother, Laurence Guarneri, runs a cookery school in Paris, so a passion for quality ingredients and good cooking has been with us from the start. We would go to the market with our mother and taste the produce straight from the farmers. And for our *goûter* (that's an after-school snack), we were never allowed sweets or fizzy drinks like the other kids – we had cheese, butter and homemade jam. We both grew up with exceptional food, but we took very different paths to becoming owners of a cheese shop.

Alex After I left university all I wanted to do was travel the world. So I took a three-month position working as a cashier at Androuet fromagerie in Paris to raise money for my travels. I ended up falling in love with cheese: the trip would have to wait. I trained as a fromager and worked in all the Androuet branches over a few years. Eventually (after some eye-opening travel), the call of English cheese became too strong to resist and I came to London to work for historic cheese merchant Paxton & Whitfield as an affineur (someone who ages and sells cheese).

Léo At school, I would come home to cook my own lunch because cafeteria food was so bland compared to what I'd grown up eating. I knew I wanted to work with food from then, so when I was offered an apprenticeship at the world-class Le Cinq restaurant at the Four Seasons George V in Paris, I jumped at the opportunity. After three years, I'd become a skilled cook, but I'd also spent time working front-of-house, learning about gold-standard service in a multi-Michelin star restaurant and five-star hotel. It was the perfect experience for setting up our own restaurant.

Our upbringing and experiences have made us passionate about cheese, passionate about seasonality and passionate about getting other people to feel like we do.

ANDROUET LONDON
AND ANDROUET FRANCE

In 2009, we decided it was time to strike out on our own. We licensed the Androuet name and set up a stall in Spitalfields Market in London, which would eventually lead to our shop and restaurant. At the beginning, we did everything ourselves. We sold the cheese, prepared the cheeseboards, dealt with orders... and our popularity grew and grew. We started supplying cheese to some of the best chefs and restaurants in London: the Galvin brothers, Duck & Waffle, Terroirs, Bruno Loubet and even the French embassy. These places are still our most valued customers.

We're the opposite of a traditional, perhaps stuffy cheese shop. There's no counter, no barrier between the cheese seller and the customer – it's open service, and that's really important to us. We want everybody to understand what seasonal cheese is – educating people is the most important part of our job.

The original Androuet was founded in 1909 on the Rue D'Amsterdam in Paris by Henri Androuet. He was the first man to travel across France to bring regional cheeses back to Paris and introduce the flavours of the mountains and the countryside to the city. He redefined the role of the fromager as not just a cheese seller, but someone who matures and cares for the cheese. In a way, Henri was the master of a revolution in flavour. After the First World War, his son Pierre joined Androuet and the business took off. Pierre travelled the world and became an authority on cheese. He wrote cookbooks and a cheese encyclopaedia, and he went on to pioneer cheese affinage techniques.

Androuet is now more successful than ever, with eight branches in Paris, two in Stockholm and one in London – each with the same seasonal philosophy, but different personalities. It's no exaggeration to say that Androuet has changed the way the people of Paris and beyond eat cheese. It's a family that we are proud to be part of.

ABOUT ALESSANDRO GRANO
AND A NOTE ON THE RECIPES

When I was growing up in Italy, there were no ready meals, no microwaves – all ingredients were fresh, seasonal and local, and that's what my grandfather (the cook of the family) would use. It's a way of cooking and eating that has stuck with me and continues to inspire me.

I started my career working as a commis chef every summer from the age of 16 while completing my culinary training. I moved to London and worked at big, glamorous hotels including The Ritz and The Dorchester, before becoming a chef de partie at the Four Seasons in Canary Wharf. But despite how exciting it was, I sometimes felt like a small part in a large machine. So I decided to work as an agency chef to get more freedom. One day, I was sent to do a simple job of preparing cheeseboards at Androuet in Spitalfields. I met Alex and Léo and quickly found we had the same approach to seasonal food. After just two days, they asked me to become their head chef.

Since then, my days have been about finding the best produce and the best producers, and never settling for what's easiest. It's just like my grandfather's food: fresh and seasonal. Now, I collaborate with cheese connoisseurs Alex and Léo, we discuss the menus together, and they have become like brothers to me.

My style is very simple. I don't like having a lot of ingredients on a plate. I like fresh flavours and I want to create tastes that make you feel at home, or that make you feel nostalgic. All the recipes in the book are things we cook in the restaurant through the seasons, and I hope that they encourage you to go and discover new flavours and exciting ways of cooking with cheese.

SPRING
GOATS' CURD, BRILLAT-SAVARIN AND THE FRESH CHEESES

Spring is about freshness. This is when goats, sheep and cows are finally let out of their barns to graze on fresh grass after a long winter of feeding on grains, scraps and hay. The difference in the quality of the milk is astonishing. The fresh grass means the milk has more minerals and vitamins, but most importantly, much more flavour.

So with fresh grass comes better milk, and with better milk comes good, fresh cheese. That means we get to eat goats' cheese like Chabichou and fresh cheeses such as Délice des Cabasses or Brillat-Savarin. These are cheeses that only mature for a few days or up to around eight weeks, so like asparagus or strawberries, their return after a long absence is welcome.

As well as super-fresh soft cheese, spring is also the time to eat the varieties that began maturing in the spring or autumn of last year. For example, you can finally indulge in hard cheese made with sheep's milk from the previous autumn, such as Ossau-Iraty, with its beautiful and subtle earthy flavours.

For producers, spring is really the beginning of the cheese cycle. This is when they start making the first harder cheeses of the year (such as the lightly aged Tomme, which will mature through the summer and be ready from around August) as well as cheeses that need to be aged much longer, but still rely on fresh milk.

ASPARAGUS WITH ROLLED ROVE DES GARRIGUES, COULIS AND SOFT-BOILED EGGS

Celebrate the arrival of asparagus in spring by pairing it with the herbaceous and light Roves des Garrigues. Start by making the coulis. Trim the asparagus and peel the woody part. Cut off the tips and set aside. Roughly chop the stems.

Put 1 tbsp of the oil in a pan over a low heat. When it's hot, add the shallot and cook until golden. Then add the chopped asparagus stems and add water to just cover. Increase the heat, bring to the boil, then reduce the heat and cook for 5 minutes until tender.

Pour the cooked shallot and asparagus in a blender with 1 Rove des Garrigues and the mint. Blend until smooth, adding more water if the coulis is too thick. Strain through a fine sieve and refrigerate while you prepare the rest of the dish.

With your fingers, make the remaining Rove des Garrigues into small balls, each the size of a hazelnut. Then roll some of the cheese balls in paprika, some in poppy seeds, some in sesame seeds and some in crushed pink peppercorns. Make sure they have an even coverage.

Next, cook the asparagus tips. Bring a pan of salted water to the boil, add the tips, reduce the heat and simmer for 2–3 minutes until tender. Remove from the heat, drain well and put in a bowl. Drizzle with the remaining oil and season with salt and pepper.

Put the eggs in a pan, cover with water and bring to the boil. Reduce the heat and cook for 6 minutes. Meanwhile, prepare a large bowl of iced water. Remove the eggs from the heat and put in the bowl of iced water for 5 minutes. Peel the eggs then cut in half.

Pour a little coulis on each plate and add a few leaves of frisée lettuce. Add the dressed asparagus tips, the cheese balls and the halved eggs. Finally, sprinkle with salt and black pepper.

SERVES 4

2 bunches of asparagus
2 tbsp olive oil
1 shallot, finely chopped
2 Roves des Garrigues
4 mint leaves
1 tbsp paprika
1 tbsp poppy seeds
1 tbsp sesame seeds
1 tbsp crushed pink
   peppercorns
4 eggs
1 head of frisée lettuce
Salt and freshly ground
   black pepper

Rove des Garrigues is made in the Provence-Alpes-Côte d'Azur region of South France. The Rove-breed goats graze on herbs and chestnuts, which gives the cheese subtle thyme, rosemary and lavender flavours.

Or look for a pasteurised, fresh, rindless goats' cheese.

SMOKED DUCK BREAST WITH BABY GEM, BRILLAT-SAVARIN AND MIXED FRESH BERRIES

SERVES 2

1 smoked duck breast
2 baby gem or romaine lettuces,
    leaves separated
40g (scant 1½oz) hazelnuts,
    toasted and crushed
80g (scant 3oz) Brillat-Savarin
100g (3½oz) mixed berries
    (raspberries, blackberries,
    blueberries)
Salt and freshly ground
    black pepper

For the dressing
4 tbsp vegetable oil
2 tbsp hazelnut oil
2 tbsp raspberry vinegar

For the fruity dressing, mix together the vegetable oil, hazelnut oil and raspberry vinegar. Add salt and pepper to taste then set aside while you prepare the rest of the salad.

Thinly slice the duck breast and put in a large bowl with the baby gem leaves and the hazelnuts. If using romaine lettuce, break the leaves into smaller pieces.

Add the dressing to the salad, mix well and divide between the serving plates.

Cut the rind from the Brillat-Savarin and break the cheese up between your fingers, then scatter it over the salad together with the berries.

Brillat-Savarin is made in the Île-de-France and Burgundy regions. It's a triple-cream cows' milk cheese with a rich texture and a hint of crème fraiche. Henri Androuet named the cheese in the 1930s after gastronome Jean Anthelme Brillat-Savarin.

Or look for a slightly lactic soft cheese with a bloomy rind.

CLACBITOU SOUFFLÉS WITH PEA COULIS

The classic soufflé is easier to cook than you might think. Start by preheating the oven to 190°C (375°F/Gas 5). Then grease 6 individual ramekins with butter and sprinkle with breadcrumbs.

Next, make a roux by putting the butter in a pan over a low heat, add the flour and stir with a whisk. Cook, stirring, for about 1 minute. Gently add the milk in parts and continue stirring until the mixture starts to thicken.

Add the grated Clacbitou and the Parmesan and stir well until the cheeses have melted. Season with salt, pepper and a few gratings of nutmeg. Remove from the heat and add the egg yolks and Dijon mustard, then transfer the mixture to a bowl.

Beat the egg whites until stiff in another bowl. Then fold one-third at a time into the cheese and egg mixture.

Put the prepared ramekins in a baking tray, then add water to the tray until three-quarters full to make a bain-marie. Divide the soufflé mixture between the ramekins, then bake for 25–30 minutes until the soufflés are well risen.

Meanwhile, make the coulis. Peel and chop the shallots and place in a pan over a medium heat with the oil. Sweat gently for 1 minute, then add 300g (11oz) peas. Just cover with water and simmer for 5 minutes, or until the peas are tender. Drain, season with salt and pepper, then whizz in a blender until smooth. If the coulis is too thick, add more water.

For the garnish, put 50g (1¾oz) peas in a pan of lightly salted boiling water and blanch for 2–3 minutes. Drain well.

When the soufflés are ready, remove and leave to cool.

Pour a little coulis on each serving plate, then unmould the soufflés and place one on each plate. Top the soufflés with some micro basil. Sprinkle with the blanched peas, the crumbled Clacbitou and some chopped chives. Drizzle with a little olive oil and serve.

SERVES 6

100g (3½oz) unsalted butter, plus extra for greasing
60g (2oz) fine fresh breadcrumbs
100g (3½oz) plain flour
600ml (1 pint) full-fat milk
180g (scant 6½oz) Clacbitou, coarsely grated
20g (¾oz) Parmesan cheese, grated
2–3 gratings of nutmeg
5 eggs, separated
20g (¾oz) Dijon mustard
Salt and freshly ground black pepper

For the coulis
100g (3½oz) shallots
2 tbsp vegetable oil
300g (11oz) fresh peas (podded weight)

To serve
50g (1¾oz) fresh peas (podded weight)
3 tbsp micro basil
20g (¾oz) Clacbitou, crumbled
1 tbsp chopped chives
2 tbsp olive oil, for drizzling

Clacbitou is made in the Burgundy region of Central France using goats' milk. It's matured with crushed garlic, seasonal herbs and parsley for a strong, aromatic, woody flavour.

Or look for a semi-soft, fresh goats' cheese matured with garlic and herbs.

GLOBE ARTICHOKES WITH DÉLICE DES CABASSES

SERVES 2

For the breadcrumbs
½ stale baguette, roughly chopped,
    or 100g (3½oz) fresh
    breadcrumbs
1 tbsp parsley
½ garlic clove
Grated zest of ½ lemon

For the artichokes
2 globe artichokes
4 tbsp olive oil, plus extra
    for drizzling
1 shallot, chopped
2 garlic cloves
1 sprig of thyme
1 bay leaf
100ml (3½fl oz) dry white wine
200g (7oz) samphire
1 hot red chilli, thinly sliced
1 Délice des Cabasses
Salt and freshly ground
    black pepper
A few semi-dried tomatoes,
    to garnish

Délice des Cabasses is a fresh curd cheese from the Midi-Pyrénées region of South France. It has a tangy, sweet flavour, a smooth texture and refreshing finish.

Or look for a fresh, smooth, pasteurised sheep's milk cheese.

To make the breadcrumbs, put the baguette or fresh breadcrumbs in a blender or food processor with the parsley, garlic and lemon zest. Blitz then set aside while you prepare the artichokes.

Start by trimming off the stem and pulling off the tough outer leaves. Spread the remaining leaves apart and pull out the innermost leaves to reveal the hairy choke. Scrape away the hairs using a teaspoon, then trim off the tops of the remaining leaves.

Put 2 tbsp olive oil in a pan over a low heat. When hot, add the chopped shallot, ½ clove garlic, the thyme and bay leaf. Sweat for 5 minutes until the shallot is translucent.

Add the artichoke hearts, season with salt and pepper and pour in the wine. Add water to cover the artichoke hearts and simmer for 10–15 minutes until the artichokes are cooked. You can test them with a toothpick; the inside should be soft but still a little firm.

Remove the artichoke hearts with a slotted spoon. Then remove the shallot, garlic and herbs with a slotted spoon and discard. Pour the remaining cooking juices into a blender and blitz with 2 tbsp olive oil until the mixture has emulsified.

To make a bed of samphire, put the samphire in a pan of boiling water and cook for 5 minutes until cooked but still crunchy. Drain, then put in a pan over a medium heat with the sliced chilli and the remaining garlic, crushed. Sauté together for a couple of minutes then leave to one side.

Preheat the grill. Put the artichoke hearts in a grill pan, divide the Délice des Cabasses between the hearts, spooning it into the middle of each. Sprinkle with the prepared breadcrumbs and drizzle with olive oil. Grill until the cheese is golden.

Divide the samphire between the serving plates, pour over the emulsified cooking juices and top with a stuffed artichoke heart. Garnish with a few semi-dried tomatoes.

FREGOLA WITH OSSAU-IRATY AND RICOTTA-STUFFED COURGETTE FLOWERS

Tend to your courgette flowers first. Carefully wipe with a damp cloth or kitchen towel, taking care not to damage them. Open the petals to reveal the bulbous pistil at the base. This is slightly bitter, so remove it by pinching or cutting it off.

Next, mix the ricotta with the lemon zest, season with salt and pepper and drizzle with a little olive oil. Put the mixture in a piping bag fitted with a plain nozzle and use to fill each flower – be careful not to fill them to bursting. Gently twist the top of the petals to close them around the mixture.

Place in a steamer and cook for 2½ minutes until tender.

To prepare the courgettes for your fregola, put 1 tbsp oil in a pan over a medium heat. When it's hot, add the courgettes, garlic and salt and pepper to taste. Sauté for a few minutes until the courgette is light golden brown but still slightly firm.

Meanwhile, make a start on the fregola, which is made much like a risotto. First, add the vegetable stock to a pan and bring to the boil. Then put the remaining oil in a large pan over a low heat. When hot, add the shallot. Cook slowly for 2–3 minutes until translucent, then add the fregola and a few pinches of salt. Stir well before adding the boiling stock, a ladleful at a time, allowing the mixture to simmer.

When the fregola is cooked but there is still some liquid in the pan, remove from the heat. Add the sautéed courgette, the cherry tomatoes, the Ossau-Iraty and the parsley and thyme. Stir until the mixture has the texture of a risotto.

Divide the fregola mixture between the serving plates and garnish each with a prepared courgette flower and a few red micro basil leaves. Drizzle with a little olive oil and serve.

SERVES 7

7 courgette flowers
250g (9½oz) sheep-milk ricotta
   or sheep-and-cows' milk ricotta
Grated zest of ½ lemon
4 tbsp olive oil, plus extra
   for drizzling
3 courgettes, finely diced
2 garlic cloves, crushed
1 litre (1¾ pints) vegetable stock
1 shallot, finely chopped
500g (1lb 2oz) fregola pasta
   (from good Italian delicatessens)
15 cherry tomatoes, halved
200g (7oz) Ossau-Iraty
A few leaves of parsley, chopped
A few sprigs of thyme, leaves only,
   chopped
Salt and freshly ground
   black pepper
Red micro basil leaves, to garnish

Ossau-Iraty is made in South-West France on the border with Spain. It can be floral and grassy when young, with a richer, nutty flavour when aged.

Or look for a hard sheep's cheese with a subtle nutty, buttery flavour.

GRILLED VEGETABLE TARTINE WITH TAPENADE AND FLEUR DU MAQUIS

SERVES 4

1 aubergine
1 courgette
1 small red onion
1 yellow pepper
1 red pepper
4 tbsp olive oil
2–3 tbsp chopped basil leaves
1 sprig of thyme, leaves only,
    chopped
400g (14oz) sourdough bread
200g (7oz) Fleur du Maquis
Salt and freshly ground
    black pepper
100g (3½oz) rocket, to garnish
Pinch of micro herbs, to garnish

For the tapenade
120g (scant 4½oz) pitted
    black kalamata or niçoise olives
½ small garlic clove
1 tbsp capers
2 tbsp olive oil
1 anchovy fillet
½ tbsp lemon juice

To prepare the vegetables, start by preheating a ridged griddle pan (you can do this the day before if you're making these for a party – they're perfect for passing round with drinks).

Cut the aubergine, courgette and red onion into 5mm (¼in) slices. Trim the yellow and red peppers, remove the pith and cut into wedges. Then season with salt and pepper and drizzle with half the olive oil.

Place the vegetables on the hot griddle pan and cook for 2 minutes, then turn them over and cook for 2 minutes more. The aubergine may require a little longer. When the vegetables are nicely blackened by the ridges of the pan remove from the pan and put in a dish. Drizzle with the remaining olive oil and add the basil and thyme. Refrigerate for a minimum of 3 hours (overnight is fine).

Next, make the tapenade. Put the olives, garlic, capers, olive oil, anchovy fillet and lemon juice in a blender or food processor and blitz to a smooth paste. Season with black pepper and set aside.

Slice the sourdough bread into four 1cm (½in) slices and toast until golden on both sides. Spread each slice with some of the tapenade and top with a pattern of grilled vegetables.

Divide the Fleur du Maquis between the slices, crumbling it on top. Flash under a hot grill for few seconds until the cheese has melted.

Garnish with rocket and micro herbs.

Fleur du Maquis is soft cheese made on the French island of Corsica. Its natural rind is covered in aromatic herbs, juniper and piquant chillies.

Or look for a soft, unpasteurised sheep's cheese, ideally with a covered rind and intense herbal flavour.

HOMEMADE FRESH CHEESE

Making your own cheese is simple and fun, and allows you to experiment with flavour – just approach the process with confidence (and a cooking thermometer!).

Start by putting the milk in a large pan over a low heat and heat slowly until it reaches 95°C (203°F), checking with a cooking thermometer.

Immediately remove from the heat, pour in the vinegar, stir and leave for 10–15 minutes until a curd floats to the surface and the whey that remains is clear.

Meanwhile, line a colander with a clean tea towel. Use a sieve to remove the curd (do this over the sink), then place the curd in the lined colander. Sprinkle with salt.

If you wish, sprinkle with the flavouring of your choice – mixed herbs, chopped thyme with lemon zest, chopped sundried tomatoes with chopped black olives, or red chilli flakes all work very well with a light, fresh cheese like this. Stir very gently to combine.

Then transfer the curd to a cheese mould or small sieve. Refrigerate in an airtight container for 3–5 days.

Serve as an antipasto or crumbled into a salad.

MAKES APPROX 400G/14 OZ

3 litres (5¼ pints) full-fat milk
90ml (3fl oz) white wine vinegar
½ tsp Maldon salt

Optional flavourings
Adjust quantities according
to taste

Mixture of chopped parsley,
    mint, rosemary and thyme
Chopped thyme with grated
    zest of lemon
Chopped sundried tomatoes
    with chopped black olives
Red chilli flakes

LAMB NAVARIN WITH SOURÉLIETTE-TOPPED TOAST

This French stew is a perfect spring supper made infinitely better by Souréliette-topped toast.

Start by cutting the lamb neck into 5cm (2in) cubes. Season well with salt and pepper. Then heat the olive oil over a medium heat in a cast-iron casserole dish. Add the lamb and brown it thoroughly all over.

Add the onion, carrots, celery, garlic and thyme. Cook, stirring, until the vegetables are lightly coloured. Add the wine, bring to the boil and cook for 2–3 minutes until the alcohol has evaporated. Add the tomatoes with their juice and stir well.

Add the stock and bring to the boil again. Reduce the heat, cover and simmer for 1½–2 hours until the meat is tender. Halfway through cooking, add the potatoes.

When the cooking time is up, season with salt and pepper, then add the peas. Cook for 5 minutes more, or until the peas are cooked. If the sauce is too thin, increase the heat and cook until the sauce has reduced and thickened.

Meanwhile, preheat the grill before preparing the Souréliette-topped toast.

To make the gremolada, mix together the lemon zest, olive oil, parsley and rosemary.

Cut the pain de campagne into 4cm (1½in) slices and drizzle with a little olive oil. Sprinkle with the grated Souréliette then place under the grill until the cheese has melted.

Serve the lamb navarin drizzled with the gremolada and with the toasted Souréliette-topped toast.

SERVES 4

800g (1¾lb) lamb neck
3 tbsp olive oil, plus extra
   for drizzling
200g (7oz) onion, chopped
200g (7oz) carrots, chopped
2 celery stalks, chopped
3 garlic cloves, chopped
1 sprig of thyme
250ml (8fl oz) dry white wine
1 x 200g (7oz) can chopped
   tomatoes in juice
600ml (1 pint) lamb or
   vegetable stock
200g (7oz) Jersey Royal potatoes,
   whole, washed and unpeeled
100g (3½oz) fresh peas
   (podded weight)
400g (14oz) pain de campagne
150g (5½oz) Souréliette, grated
Salt and freshly ground
   black pepper

For the gremolada
Grated zest of 1 lemon
2 tbsp olive oil
A few leaves of chopped parsley
1 sprig of rosemary, chopped

Souréliette is made in the Midi-Pyrénées region of South France from sheep's milk. It has a fruity, fresh-hazelnut flavour.

Or look for a semi-hard mountain cheese with a fruity flavour.

SPICED LAMB RUMP WITH AUBERGINE CAVIAR, CRUSHED POTATO, TOMATO CONFIT AND YOGURT TZATZIKI

SERVES 2

1 tsp coriander seed
1 tbsp cumin seed
1 whole cardamom
½ tsp caraway seeds
2 lamb rumps
2 tbsp olive oil, plus extra for
   drizzling
300g (11oz) desiree potatoes
20g (¾oz) black olives, roughly
   chopped
Salt and freshly ground black
   pepper
A few mint leaves, to garnish

For the tomato confit
6 cherry tomatoes
250ml (8fl oz) (approx) olive oil
Grated zest of 1 lemon
1 sprig of thyme, leaves only

For the tzatziki
1 cucumber
120g (scant 4½oz) goats' milk
   yogurt
1 tbsp chopped mint
½ garlic clove, finely chopped
juice of ½ lemon
1 tbsp olive oil

For the aubergine caviar
1 aubergine
2 tbsp olive oil, plus extra for
   drizzling
2 sprigs of thyme, leaves only
1 garlic clove, crushed
1 plum tomato
Tip of 1 red bird's eye chilli,
   deseeded
1 tbsp chopped parsley
Juice of ½ lemon

It's best to make the tomato confit and the tzatziki the day before you want to serve this dish, because the tomato for the confit needs to spend long hours in the oven. And if you want perfect cucumber for your tzatziki, you need to salt it and drain it overnight. Also, think about prepping your lamb several hours in advance. It's all worth it!

For the confit, start by preheating the oven to the lowest possible temperature.

Score the skin of the cherry tomatoes a couple of times. Put in a bowl of boiling water for few seconds and then in a bowl of iced water. Remove the skin, then put in a baking tray with enough olive oil to come halfway up the tomatoes. Add the lemon zest and thyme leaves, and season with salt and pepper.

Bake in the oven for 6–7 hours until slightly soft. If this seems laborious, you can make a larger quantity of confit and keep it refrigerated, covered with olive oil in a jar, for up to 2 weeks.

For the tzatziki, peel and deseed the cucumber. Put in a colander with a pinch of salt and leave overnight so the excess moisture in the cucumber drains and does not dilute the finished tzatziki.

The next day, rinse the salt from the cucumber and leave to drain. Put the drained cucumber in a bowl, and add the yogurt, mint, garlic, lemon juice and olive oil. Season with salt and pepper and set aside.

Crush the coriander seed, cumin seed, cardamom and caraway seeds in a mortar. Season with salt and pepper, drizzle with a little olive oil, and rub well over the lamb. Refrigerate, covered, for 4 hours.

Half an hour before cooking, remove the lamb from the fridge and leave to stand at room temperature.

Continued overleaf

Meanwhile, make the aubergine caviar. Preheat the oven to 180°C (350°F/Gas 4).

Cut the aubergine in half and put in a baking tray. Score with a knife, season with salt and pepper and drizzle with a little olive oil. Add the thyme leaves and garlic. Cover with foil and bake for 20 minutes, then remove the foil and return to the oven for 10–15 minutes more, or until the aubergine is soft.

Remove the pulp with a spoon and chop it roughly. Put in a colander over a bowl and leave until the excess juice has drained.

Cut the tomato in half and deseed it. Chop the tomato and the chilli and mix with the aubergine caviar. Add the chopped parsley, lemon juice and the remaining 2 tbsp olive oil. Season with salt and pepper and set the caviar aside.

Next, make your crushed potatoes. Start by peeling the potatoes, cut them into chunks and put in a pan of cold, salted water. Bring to the boil then reduce the heat and simmer for 10–15 minutes until tender. Drain well, return to the pan and crush with a fork. Add the chopped black olives, season with salt and pepper and stir in 2 tbsp olive oil. Set aside.

Preheat the oven to 180°C (350°F/Gas 4). Heat a roasting pan over a medium heat and when it is very hot, add the lamb. Sear the lamb all over until golden brown, then put in the oven for 10–15 minutes to cook to medium.

Remove from the oven and leave to rest for 2–3 minutes, then cut each rump into 2 slices.

Put some crushed potato on each plate and top with the sliced lamb. Use two spoons to make quenelles from the aubergine caviar and put one quenelle on each plate. Add a few spoonfuls of tzatziki and some tomato confit. Garnish with a few mint leaves and serve.

Goats' milk yogurt is creamy and slightly sweet with a tangy finish. It's best to buy it from a good fromagerie, as it will be free from additives and artificial flavourings.

PASTA ROLLS WITH BROUSSE AND SUNDRIED TOMATOES

This beautifully cheesy dish is great for informal dinner parties.

If you're making your own pasta dough, put the oo flour, semolina flour, eggs and a pinch of salt in a food processor. Blitz until the mixture resembles coarse breadcrumbs. Put the mixture on a clean work surface, gather it together with your hands and knead with your palm for about 10 minutes to make a smooth, shiny dough. Cover with cling film and put in a cool place for 1 hour.

Cut the dough in half. Roll each half into a very thin sheet about 30cm (12in) long. A rolling pin is fine, a pasta machine is better. If using a pasta machine, set the rollers to their widest position and dust lightly with flour. Feed the dough through the rollers. Repeat several times, each time setting the rollers closer together until the dough is the right length and thickness. Cover with a clean tea towel to avoid drying out.

Bring a large pan of salted water to the boil over a high heat and add each pasta sheet one at a time. Cook for 3–4 minutes until al dente. Drain in a colander, taking care not to break the sheets. Leave to dry on 2 clean tea towels.

Meanwhile, make the filling. In a bowl mix together the Brousse, olives, sundried tomatoes, pine kernels, Parmesan, oil, basil, and salt and pepper to taste.

Leaving the sheets of pasta on tea towels, divide the filling between each sheet, spreading to a thickness of about 5mm (¼in). Use the tea towel to roll up the pasta and its filling, creating 2 rolls. Cut each roll into 2cm (¾in) slices. Put in an oiled grill pan, sprinkle with a little Parmesan and drizzle with a little oil. Place under the grill until lightly browned.

For the tomato sauce, heat the oil in a pan over a medium heat. Add the garlic and cook for a couple of minutes. Add the tomatoes and sauté until slightly soft. Add the basil, then season with salt and pepper.

Serve the pasta rolls accompanied by the tomato sauce.

SERVES 8

160g (5½oz) Parmesan, grated
3 tbsp olive oil, plus extra for drizzling
Salt and freshly ground black pepper

For the pasta dough
340g (12oz) oo flour, plus extra for dusting
160g (5½oz) semolina flour
5 eggs

For the filling
500g (1lb 2oz) Brousse
1 tbsp black olives, pitted and chopped
2 tbsp sundried tomatoes, chopped
1 tsp toasted pine kernels
10g (¼oz) Parmesan
2 tbsp olive oil
6 basil leaves, chopped

For the sauce
2 tbsp olive oil
1 garlic clove, crushed
200g (7oz) cherry tomatoes, halved
6 basil leaves, torn

Brousse is made in the Provence-Alpes-Côte d'Azur region of South France from sheep's milk. It's a fresh, light curd cheese with a hint of freshly cut grass.

Or look for a mild, soft, low-fat, fresh cheese with a slightly salty flavour.

ROAST BEETROOT, GOATS' CURD AND PINE KERNEL SALAD

SERVES 2

500g (1lb 2oz) mixed variety of
   beetroot, unpeeled
1 orange, unpeeled and cut
   into wedges
A few sprigs of thyme
2 garlic cloves, crushed
2 tbsp olive oil
Grated zest of ½ lemon
Handful of rocket
160g (5½oz) goats' curd
1 tbsp toasted pine kernels
Salt and freshly ground
   black pepper

For the dressing
2 tbsp cider vinegar
4 tbsp vegetable oil
2 tbsp olive oil
1 tsp honey
A few thyme leaves

This is an ideal dish to make the day before a lunch date as the marinated beetroot is best when left in the fridge overnight.

The day before you want to serve, preheat the oven to 190°C (375°F/Gas 5) and line a baking tray with foil.

Thoroughly wash the beetroots and place in the prepared baking tray. Add the orange wedges, a few sprigs of thyme and the crushed garlic cloves. Drizzle with the oil.

Cover with more foil and fold the edges together to make a loose parcel, then bake for 40–60 minutes, depending on the size of the beetroots.

To check they are cooked, pierce them through the unopened foil with a toothpick; if the toothpick goes in without meeting any resistance, the beetroots are ready. Remove from the oven and leave to cool in the foil.

Meanwhile, make the dressing: put the vinegar, vegetable oil, olive oil and honey in a bowl and whisk together well. Season with salt and pepper and add a few thyme leaves.

Peel the cooled beetroots and cut into wedges, then place them in a dish and sprinkle with the lemon zest and only half of the dressing. Refrigerate overnight, covered with cling film.

Ten minutes before serving, remove the beetroots from the fridge.

Divide the rocket between the serving plates, then add the beetroot and spoonfuls of goats' curd. Scatter with the pine kernels, drizzle with the remaining dressing and serve.

Goats' curd is a soft, fresh, light cheese with a creamy texture and a slightly tangy and sweet finish.

CHABICHOU DU POITOU RÖSTIS WITH GIROLLES AND POACHED DUCK EGGS

SERVES 6

500g (1lb 2oz) fresh girolle
    mushrooms
100ml (3½fl oz) vegetable oil
Splash of white balsamic vinegar
Splash of white wine vinegar
6 duck eggs
Salt and freshly ground black
    pepper
A few leaves of micro cress,
    to garnish

For the röstis
50g (1¾oz) unsalted butter
100g (3½oz) onions, finely sliced
300g (11oz) desiree potatoes
125g (4½oz) Chabichou du Poitou,
    grated
1 tbsp chopped dill
30g (1oz) spinach leaves,
    finely sliced
2 spring onions, sliced
1 egg

For the truffle mayonnaise
1 egg yolk
1 tsp white wine vinegar
100ml (3½fl oz) vegetable oil
1 tsp black truffle paste or
    black truffle oil

Chabichou du Poitou is made
in the Poitou-Charentes region
of West France and dates back
to the eighth century. The
medium goats' cheese has a
characteristically wrinkly rind.

Or look for a fresh and zesty
goats' cheese.

Start by making the truffle mayonnaise. Put the egg yolk and
wine vinegar in a food mixer and start mixing together slowly,
then gradually add the oil in a thin stream.

As the mayonnaise thickens, gradually increase the speed.
When the mayonnaise is thick and silky, season with salt and
black pepper, then add the truffle paste or oil. Refrigerate
while you prepare the rest of the dish.

For the röstis, put the butter in a pan over a medium heat.
When the butter has melted, add the onion and cook until
golden brown. Remove from the heat and set aside.

Peel and grate the potatoes and put in a bowl with the
Chabichou du Poitou, the dill, spinach, spring onion, egg and
cooked onion. Mix well and season with salt and pepper.

Preheat the oven to 180°C (350°F/Gas 4).

Using a food ring or a spoon, make 6 röstis from the rösti
mixture in a baking tray. Bake for 15 minutes until they have
a nice crust.

Meanwhile, thoroughly clean the girolles of any dirt, and if
they are large, cut in half. Put the oil in a pan over a medium
heat and when it's hot, add the girolles. Sauté for few minutes
but do not allow to colour, then add the balsamic vinegar
and season.

Finally, to poach the eggs, bring some water to the boil in
a pan, then add a splash of wine vinegar. Stir the water
vigorously, then break the duck eggs and add them to the
water, one at a time. Simmer for about 3 minutes until firm
outside but still soft inside. Carefully remove with a slotted
spoon and drain on kitchen towel.

Place a rösti on each serving plate and top with a poached egg.
Season with salt and cracked black pepper. Divide the girolles
between the plates and drizzle with the truffle mayonnaise.
Garnish with a few leaves of micro cress.

'CIGARS' WITH BROUSSE

These brick/filo pastry rolls are delicious served warm, and make simple snack-sized starters for lunch or dinner.

To make the filling, put 1 tbsp olive oil in a pan over a medium heat. Add the onion and garlic and cook, stirring, for a few minutes. When the onion is translucent, remove from the heat.

Put the Brousse, parsley, dill, coriander, flour, eggs and raisins in a bowl and mix until well combined. Add the pine kernels and the cooked onion and garlic mixture. Mix well then season with nutmeg, salt and pepper.

Preheat the oven to 200°C (400°F/Gas 6).

Place a brick/filo pastry sheet on the work surface and cut it in half. Brush each half with a little olive oil then place a spoonful of the cheese mixture in the centre. Roll the pastry up like a cigar.

Bake for 10 minutes until the 'cigars' are golden brown.

1 tbsp olive oil, plus extra
   for brushing
1 onion, finely chopped
1 garlic clove, finely chopped
250g (9½oz) Brousse
1 tbsp each of chopped parsley,
   dill, coriander
2 tbsp plain flour
2 eggs
50g (1¾oz) raisins
80g (scant 3oz) toasted
   pine kernels
2–3 gratings of nutmeg
12 sheets of brick pastry or
   filo pastry
Salt and freshly ground
   black pepper

Brousse is made in the Provence-Alpes-Côte d'Azur region of South France from sheep's milk. It's a fresh, light curd cheese with a hint of freshly cut grass.

Or look for A mild, soft, low-fat, fresh cheese with a slightly salty flavour.

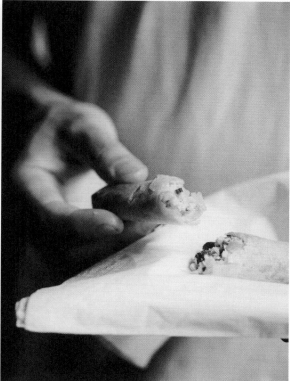

BRILLAT-SAVARIN CHEESECAKE WITH MARINATED CHERRIES

The rich Brillat-Savarin guarantees a perfectly indulgent cheesecake.

Start by whipping the cream to soft peak stage, then refrigerate. Meanwhile, put the sugar and eggs in a mixing bowl and beat until the sugar has dissolved. Add the Brillat-Savarin, lemon zest and vanilla seeds and mix well until completely smooth.

Next, 'bloom' the gelatine by putting it in a small bowl of cold water and leaving it for 1 minute until it is soft. Remove the gelatine from the bowl and press it between your fingers to squeeze out the excess water. Place in a small bowl and microwave for 2–3 seconds on a regular setting, until liquid. Add the liquid gelatine to the cheese mixture and stir well. Then gently fold in the whipped cream.

To make the base, roughly crush the biscuits. Put the butter in a pan over a low heat, and when it has melted add to the crushed biscuits. Mix together thoroughly.

Place five 7cm (2¾in) cooking rings or one 20cm (8in) ring on a baking tray. Line the rings with a strip of baking parchment cut to the same depth as the ring.

Distribute the crushed biscuits between the rings and press down well with a spoon. Gently pour the cheese mixture over the biscuits, leaving a 5mm (¼in) space at the top. Refrigerate for a minimum of 5 hours.

To make the decorative marinated cherries, cut them in half and remove the stones. Put the chopped mint in a bowl with the cherries and cassis. Mix together thoroughly. Cover with cling film and place in the fridge to marinate.

For the glaze, melt the jam in a small pan with the water. Remove from the heat and pass through a fine sieve. Leave to cool for 10 minutes, then pour the glaze on the cheesecakes in a thin layer. Refrigerate for 1 hour until set.

SERVES 5

200ml (7fl oz) whipping cream
70g (2oz) caster sugar
2 eggs
175g (6oz) Brillat-Savarin
Grated zest of ½ lemon
Seeds from ½ vanilla pod
5g gold leaf gelatine
100g (3½oz) digestive biscuits
40g (scant 1½oz) unsalted butter
200g (7oz) fresh cherries
1 tsp finely chopped mint,
    plus a few leaves, to decorate
7 tsp cassis
100g (3½oz) morello cherry jam
2 tbsp water

Brillat-Savarin is made in the Île-de-France and Burgundy regions. It's a triple cream cows' milk cheese with a rich texture and a hint of crème fraiche. Henri Androuet named the cheese in the 1930s after gastronome Jean Anthelme Brillat-Savarin.

Or look for a slightly lactic soft cheese with a bloomy rind.

BLANCMANGE, RHUBARB AND CHAMPAGNE AND ALMOND CRUMBLE

SERVES 6

For the blancmange
400g (14oz) fromage blanc
200g (7oz) condensed milk
5g gold leaf gelatine
200ml (7fl oz) whipping cream

For the rhubarb
150g (5½oz) rhubarb
2 tbsp caster sugar
60ml (2fl oz) champagne
1 vanilla pod

For the almond crumble
150g (5½oz) plain flour
100g (3½oz) unsalted butter
85g (3oz) caster sugar
Pinch of salt
50g (1¾oz) chopped almonds

Fromage blanc is a fresh cows' milk cheese with a sweet and slightly tart flavour. Its texture is thicker than stirred yogurt. It's best to buy it from a good fromagerie, as it will be free from additives and artificial flavourings.

For the blancmange, mix together the fromage blanc and condensed milk in a large bowl.

'Bloom' the gelatine by putting it in a small bowl of cold water and leaving it for 1 minute until it is soft. Remove the gelatine from the bowl and press it between your fingers to squeeze out the excess water.

Put half the cream in a pan over a low heat and warm it gently. Remove from the heat, then add the softened gelatine and mix well until the gelatine has dissolved. Add the remaining cream and mix well.

Gently fold the gelatine mixture into the fromage blanc mixture.

Divide between 6 individual moulds and then refrigerate for a minimum of 4 hours until firm.

Meanwhile, prepare the rhubarb. Cut into small dice and place in a pan over a medium heat with the sugar, champagne and vanilla pod. Bring to the boil, then reduce the heat and simmer for 5 minutes until the rhubarb is soft but still firm. Discard the vanilla pod, then refrigerate.

For the almond crumble, preheat the oven to 170°C (325°F/Gas 3). Then put the flour, butter, sugar, salt and almonds in a bowl and rub together with your fingertips until the mixture resembles coarse breadcrumbs.

Spread on a baking sheet and bake in the oven for 15–20 minutes, stirring the mixture from time to time. When golden brown, remove from the oven and leave to cool.

To serve, run hot water over the outside of the moulds to remove the blancmange,s and then tip out on to a plate. Top with a little almond crumble, add some rhubarb and its juice on the side, and serve.

SPRING
CHEESEBOARD

Fourme d'Ambert
A mild, blue-veined cows' cheese from Auvergne with a firm, smooth texture (see p85)

Rove des Garrigues
A beautiful fresh goats' cheese from Provence-Alpes-Côte d'Azur with subtle thyme, rosemary and lavender flavours (see p32)

Camembert
An earthy, rich and fruity soft cows' cheese from Normandy (see p134)

Pave d'Auge
A holey, soft cows' cheese from Normandy with a strong, spicy flavour and a washed rind

Westcombe Cheddar
A hard English cows' cheese with nutty, sweet flavours and a lingering finish (see p112)

SUMMER
RICOTTA, MOZZARELLA AND THE SOFT CHEESES

Overleaf: Reblochon de Savoie (which makes use of summer cows' milk) maturing in caves

Summer is the best time of year for cheese. The animals are outside grazing on fresh grass and producers can achieve some of the best-quality milk of the year.

Throughout summer, you'll be eating the finest blue cheeses made from spring milk that have been ageing for around three months, such as an early Fourme d'Ambert which will still be full of fresh notes at this time.

Another one of our favourites in summer is Saint Nicolas de la Dalmerie, produced by orthodox monks in Herault (in the south of France) only in spring and summer. The flavour of the milk is beautiful from the beginning of summer. We are always very excited when we receive a message from Father Gabriel at the monastery announcing that production is starting again.

Cheeses that are produced all year around, such as Ricotta and Mozzarella, are at their best in summer. Ricotta only matures for around two weeks, so when it's made with July and August milk, it's especially aromatic and delicious. Similarly, Mozzarella matures for two to three weeks, so using summer milk means it tastes even fresher and more milky.

Summer is also the time that Alpine cheese (produced in the high mountains) goes into production, from the end of June until the middle of September. Alpine cheese (such as Gruyère) is characterised by the outstanding quality of the grass and the varieties of wild flowers the animals graze on, and it can be enjoyed from autumn.

AUBERGINE, CONFIT TOMATO AND ST TOLA TERRINE

This terrine sets in the fridge overnight, so prepare the day before required.

Start with the confit tomatoes. Preheat the oven to the lowest temperature. Then score the skin of the tomatoes a couple of times. Put in a bowl of boiling water for 10 seconds and then in a bowl of iced water. Remove the skin, deseed and cut in 4.

Put in a baking tray, sprinkle with the sugar and thyme, season with salt and pepper, and drizzle with oil. Bake in the oven for 1½ hours. Remove, then leave to cool.

For the aubergine caviar, increase the oven temperature to 190°C (375°F/Gas 5). Put the whole aubergines in the oven and bake for 1 hour. They are cooked when a toothpick goes in without meeting any resistance. Remove, then leave to cool before cutting it in half. Use a spoon to remove the pulp, then put it in a food processor and blitz for few seconds.

'Bloom' the gelatine by putting it in a small bowl of cold water and leaving for 1 minute until it is soft. Remove the gelatine from the bowl and press it between your fingers to squeeze out the excess water. Place in a small bowl in a microwave for 2–3 seconds until liquid.

Put the aubergine purée in a bowl with the olives, capers, tomato, lemon juice, parsley and basil. Add the gelatine and season with salt and pepper. Mix together thoroughly.

Line a 20cm (8in) terrine tin with cling film, leaving enough cling film hanging over the edges to fold over the top. Put half the aubergine caviar mixture in the tin, then cover with half the confit tomatoes and half the St Tola. Repeat with another layer of aubergine caviar, followed by the remaining confit tomatoes and St Tola. Fold the cling film over to cover, then refrigerate overnight.

The next day, open the cling film, put a plate on top of the terrine tin and turn the terrine out. Slice with a sharp knife and serve with some baby leaf salad and a drizzle of olive oil.

SERVES 12

350g (12oz) St Tola, cut into 5mm (¼in) slices
Salt and freshly ground black pepper
500g (1lb 2oz) baby leaf salad, to serve
Olive oil, to serve

For the confit tomatoes
20 plum tomatoes
2 level tbsp demerara sugar
4 sprigs of thyme, leaves only
Olive oil, for drizzling

For the aubergine caviar
6 aubergines
8g gold leaf gelatine
60g (2oz) pitted black olives, finely chopped
20g (¾oz) capers, finely chopped
1 plum tomato, deseeded and chopped
Juice of 1 lemon
1 tbsp chopped parsley
1 tbsp chopped basil leaves

St Tola in made in County Clare in West Ireland using goats' milk. The Saanen, Toggenburg and British Alpine goats graze on herbs and wild flowers.

Or look for a smooth, creamy goats' cheese with a mild, nutty flavour.

GREEN AND WHITE ASPARAGUS WITH RED LEICESTER CRISPS AND SAUCE VIERGE

Using both green and white asparagus gives a lovely visual contrast on the plate as well as providing subtly different flavours.

For the sauce vierge, cut the tomatoes in half, scoop out the seeds, then cut the flesh into small cubes. Put in a bowl with the chervil, parsley, shallot, lemon juice and oil and season with salt and pepper.

Next, wash the green asparagus and peel the white asparagus (as white asparagus tends to be tougher).

In a pan, bring some salted water to the boil and add the white asparagus. Blanch for 2 minutes, then add the green asparagus and blanch for 2–3 minutes more until tender. Drain and place in a bowl, then season with black pepper.

While the asparagus is cooking, put a dry non-stick pan over a medium heat. When it's hot, sprinkle over the grated Red Leicester in a thin layer in a circle about 10cm (4in) in diameter. Cook until crispy. Using a spatula, remove to kitchen paper and leave to cool.

Divide the asparagus between the serving plates and top with a crisp. Serve accompanied by the sauce vierge.

SERVES 6 (STARTER)

1 bunch of green asparagus
1 bunch of white asparagus
100g (3½oz) Red Leicester, grated
Salt and freshly ground
    black pepper

For the sauce vierge
3 plum tomatoes
½ tbsp finely chopped chervil
½ tbsp finely chopped parsley
1 shallot, finely chopped
Juice of ½ lemon
2 tbsp olive oil

Red Leicester is made in the county of Leicestershire in the Midlands in England. It's made from cows' milk, and has a crumbly, leathery texture and tangy finish.

Or look for a hard, pressed cows' cheese with robust flavour.

BABY SPINACH, CHORIZO AND MANCHEGO SALAD WITH SOFT-BOILED EGGS

2 eggs
250g (9½oz) cooking chorizo
    (dulce or piccante)
250g (9½oz) baby spinach leaves
80g (scant 3oz) aged Manchego,
    shaved
Salt and freshly ground
    black pepper

For the dressing
6 tbsp olive oil
2 tbsp sherry vinegar
½ shallot, finely chopped
½ garlic clove, finely chopped
A few tarragon leaves,
    finely chopped
A few basil leaves, finely chopped

Punchy chorizo, comforting eggs and nutty Manchego combine beautifully in this sunny-day lunch dish.

Ideally, you should prepare the dressing the day before in order for the flavours to really marry.

Put the oil, vinegar, shallot, garlic, tarragon and basil in a bowl. Mix well and season with salt and pepper, then cover with cling film and refrigerate overnight.

The next day, put the eggs in a pan with water to cover. Bring to boil, then reduce the heat and cook for 6 minutes. Remove from the pan and place in iced water for a few minutes. Peel the eggs and cut in half.

Cut the chorizo into 2cm (¾in) slices. Put in a dry frying pan over a medium heat and sauté, turning frequently, until it is golden brown and crispy outside. Remove with a slotted spoon.

Put the spinach in a bowl with the sautéed chorizo. Add the dressing and toss together well. Add the soft-boiled eggs and plenty of Manchego shavings. Serve with a bit of crusty bread.

Manchego is made in the La Mancha region of Central Spain where Manchega-breed sheep graze on an arid, rocky terrain. It can have a mild chestnut flavour when young, with a more intense flavour that lingers on the palate when aged.

Or look for an aged Manchego or a firm sheep's cheese with a chestnut flavour.

BUFFALO MOZZARELLA WITH PICKLED BABY AUBERGINE AND RED PEPPER COULIS

To get a proper pickle, you need to prepare the baby aubergines at least a week before you need them.

Start by cutting the aubergines in half and score the flesh several times with a knife. Put in a dish, sprinkle with salt and refrigerate for 4 hours. Remove from the fridge, rinse and pat dry with kitchen paper.

Put the vinegar and water in a large pan and bring to the boil. Add the aubergine halves, reduce the heat and cook for 8 minutes, until you can pierce the skin with a toothpick.

Remove with a slotted spoon to a clean kitchen towel and leave to cool. When cool, put in a jar with the garlic, chilli and bay leaves. Then cover with olive oil and refrigerate for 1 week. The pickled aubergine will keep in the fridge for at least 1 month.

For the pepper coulis, either preheat the oven to 200°C (400°F/Gas 6) or preheat the grill. Place the whole pepper in the oven or in the grill pan and cook for 15 minutes until the skin is peeling off. Remove from the heat and leave to cool. Peel and deseed. Then put in a blender with the basil leaves, tomato and garlic. Blend to a purée.

Put a little pepper coulis on each serving plate. Crumble the Mozzarella on top and sprinkle with a few rocket leaves. Add some pickled aubergine and a few black olives and caperberries.

SERVES 4

2 x 125g (4½oz) Buffalo Mozzarella
Handful of rocket
8 black olives
8 caperberries
Salt

For the pickled aubergine
500g (1lb 2oz) baby aubergines
500ml (16fl oz) white wine vinegar
500ml (16fl oz) water
1 garlic clove
1 hot red chilli
3 bay leaves
250ml (8fl oz) olive oil

For the pepper coulis
1 red pepper
2 basil leaves
1 plum tomato, cut in half
    and deseeded
½ garlic clove

Buffalo Mozzarella is made in the Campania region of South Italy from the rich, fatty milk of water buffalo.

Or look for a light and tangy buffalo milk cheese with a delicate, pillowy texture.

CHILLED TOMATO SOUP WITH RICOTTA AND BASIL OIL

SERVES 6

1kg (2¼lb) ripe plum tomatoes
60g (2oz) demerara sugar
8 tbsp peppery extra virgin
    olive oil
1 large red onion
2 celery sticks
2 garlic cloves
2 tbsp balsamic vinegar
2 sprigs of basil, leaves only
1 sprig of thyme
500ml (16fl oz) fresh tomato juice
Salt and freshly ground
    black pepper

To serve
250g (9½oz) Ricotta
20g (¾oz) black olives, pitted
6 caperberries
Micro basil

For the basil oil
150g (5½oz) basil leaves
300ml (10fl oz) vegetable oil
100ml (3½fl oz) olive oil

Ricotta is made in Italy: broadly using sheep's milk in the south of the country and cows' milk in the north.

Or look for a fresh, mild curd cheese with a sweet, earthy and slightly acidic flavour.

The basil oil in this recipe will keep in the fridge for 6 months, so it's ideal to make in advance and use for other dishes such as bruschetta or salads, or with salmon.

To prepare it, put the basil in a blender or food processor with the vegetable oil and olive oil. Blitz for few seconds, then put in a pan over a medium heat. Using a thermometer, heat to 70°C (158°F). Continue heating for 3–4 minutes, keeping the mixture at this temperature. Remove from the heat and leave to cool.

When cool, strain into a bowl through a fine sieve, then transfer to a bottle or jar and refrigerate until you need it.

For the soup, preheat the oven to 190°C (375°F/Gas 5).

Cut the tomatoes in half and place on a baking tray. Sprinkle with the sugar, drizzle with a little olive oil and season with salt and pepper. Bake for 15-20 minutes until soft, then remove from the oven and set aside.

Cut the onion, celery and garlic into chunks. Put 2 tbsp oil in a pan over a medium heat and when it's hot, add the chunks. Reduce the heat and sweat for 5 minutes, until lightly coloured, then season with salt.

Put the roasted tomatoes, sweated vegetables, vinegar, basil, thyme and tomato juice in a bowl. If you have time or are making this in advance, you should cover the bowl with cling film and refrigerate overnight – the chilling allows the flavours to blend. But if you are in a rush, just omit this step.

Put the tomato mixture in a blender and blend until smooth. Add the remaining oil and blend again until the soup is emulsified. Season with salt and pepper.

Divide the soup between the serving bowls. Add a spoonful of ricotta and a drizzle of basil oil to each bowl. Garnish with olives, caperberries and micro basil.

CROTTIN DE CHAVIGNOL SALAD WITH CARAMELISED WALNUTS

2 Crottins de Chavignol
2 tbsp clear honey
2 tbsp thyme leaves
Handful of mixed leaf salad
2 tbsp sundried tomatoes
Salt and freshly ground
  black pepper

For the caramelised walnuts
100g (3½oz) walnuts
1 tsp demerara sugar
1½ tbsp clear honey
Pinch of dried herbes de Provence
1 tsp unsalted butter, room
  temperature

For the dressing
3 tbsp olive oil
3 tbsp vegetable oil
2 tbsp sherry vinegar
1 tsp clear honey
1 tsp wholegrain mustard

This uncomplicated salad makes for an impressive lunch dish, with the caramelised walnut pairing divinely with the warm Crottin de Chavignol.

For the caramelised walnuts, preheat the oven to 170°C (325°F/Gas 3).

Then mix together the walnuts, sugar, honey and herbes de Provence before spreading on a baking tray. Bake for 20 minutes or until the nuts are a caramel colour.

Remove from the oven and mix with the butter. Leave to cool, taking care that the walnuts stay separate. Set aside.

For the dressing, whisk together the olive oil and vegetable oil, the vinegar, honey and mustard, and then season with salt and pepper.

Slice the Crottins de Chavignol, drizzle with a little honey and put under a preheated grill until the cheese has caramelised. Sprinkle with thyme leaves.

Toss the salad in the dressing and divide between the serving plates. Add a caramelised crottin to each plate. Crumble over some caramelised walnuts and sprinkle with sundried tomatoes.

Crottin de Chavignol is made in the Sancerre region of Central France. It's a firm goats' cheese which can be crumbled, and has a mild flowery and earthy flavour.

Or look for a creamy, rich, pasteurised goats' cheese.

FETA AND WATERMELON SALAD

Tangy, just-pickled red onions elevate this classic summer salad into something special, so it's worth preparing the day before – or at least few hours ahead of serving.

To prepare, cut the onion into small wedges, rinse under cold water and put in a bowl. Sprinkle with salt and pepper and cover with the red wine vinegar. Refrigerate for 5 hours or overnight.

For the rest of the salad, peel the watermelon, cut into cubes and place in a bowl. Cut the cucumber in half and scrape out the seeds. Cut into cubes and add to the watermelon. Crumble over the Feta.

Season with salt and pepper, lemon juice and oil. Add the mint and oregano.

Thoroughly drain the red onion and add to the bowl together with the olives. Toss the salad and scatter with thyme leaves and decorate with mini courgette flowers, if using.

SERVES 4

1 red onion
200ml (7fl oz) red wine vinegar
500g (1lb 2oz) watermelon
1 cucumber
200g (7oz) Feta
Juice of 1 lemon
3 tbsp olive oil
4 mint leaves, finely chopped
2 pinches of oregano leaves
12 kalamata olives, pitted
½ tsp thyme leaves
Salt and freshly ground
    black pepper
Mini courgette flowers,
    to garnish (optional)

Feta in made in Greece. It's a fresh curd cheese traditionally aged in beechwood barrels. It has a fragile, crumbly texture and a citrus, spicy flavour.

Or look for a fresh, firm, sheep's milk cheese with an acidic flavour.

FOURME D'AMBERT DIP WITH CRUDITÉS

SERVES 6

1 large carrot
1 cucumber
2 celery sticks
1 bunch of radishes
Salt and freshly ground
   black pepper
Toasted baguette, to serve

For the dip
100g (3½oz) Fourme d'Ambert
100g (3½oz) fromage blanc
100g (3½oz) crème fraîche
1 tbsp sherry vinegar
½ garlic clove, finely chopped
1 tbsp finely chopped chervil
1 tbsp finely chopped chives
Olive oil, for drizzling

An effortless but high-impact dip.

First, put the Fourme d'Ambert, fromage blanc, crème fraîche, vinegar and garlic in a food processor. Blend to a smooth consistency, then season to taste with salt and pepper. Stir in the chervil and chives. Place in a small bowl and set aside while you prepare the crudités.

Peel the carrot, cut in quarters lengthways and remove the core. Cut into 10cm (4in) lengths. Repeat with the cucumber but do not peel. Cut the celery into matchsticks about 10cm (4in) long, but do not trim off the leaves. Wash and trim the radishes.

When you are ready to serve, drizzle the dip with a little olive oil and serve with the crudités and some toasted baguette.

Fourme d'Ambert is made in the Auvergne region of Central France from cows' milk and dates back to the Middle Ages. It's a mild, firm, blue-veined cheese which becomes more robust with age.

Or look for a soft, mild, young blue cheese.

HADDOCK AND OGLESHIELD FISHCAKES WITH BROWN SHRIMP SAUCE

SERVES 4 (STARTER) OR 2 (MAIN)

200g (7oz) desiree potatoes
300g (11oz) haddock
200ml (7fl oz) full-fat milk
400ml (14fl oz) water
1 small onion
1 bay leaf
4–5 black peppercorns
1 tbsp chopped dill
1 tbsp chopped parsley
50g (1¾oz) Ogleshield, grated
30g (1oz) spring onion, sliced
1 egg
½ tbsp Dijon mustard
5 tbsp vegetable oil
100ml (3½fl oz) double cream
Juice of 1 lemon
½ tbsp capers
60g (2oz) brown shrimps
1 tbsp chopped parsley
Salt and freshly ground
  black pepper
3 small handfuls of watercress,
  to garnish

Ogleshield is made in the county of Somerset in South West England using raw Jersey cows' milk. It has a creamy, rich and fruity flavour.

Or look for a hard, pressed cows' cheese similar to Raclette (see p110).

Start by preparing the potatoes for the fishcakes. Preheat the oven to 190°C (375°F/Gas 5).

Put the whole potatoes in a roasting tin. Cover with foil and bake for 50–60 minutes, or until soft. Remove from the oven, leave until cool enough to handle, then peel. While still warm, pass through a medium sieve and leave to one side.

Next, poach the fish. Put the haddock in a large pan over a medium heat. Cover with the milk and water, then add half the onion, the bay leaf and the peppercorns. Bring to boil, then reduce the heat and simmer for 3–4 minutes, until the haddock is soft but not overcooked. Strain and set aside. Discard the cooking juices, skin, bones, onion, bay leaf and peppercorns.

Put the sieved potatoes in a bowl with the dill and parsley, Ogleshield, spring onion, egg and mustard. Season with salt and pepper but do not oversalt as the cheese adds its own saltiness. Add the cooked haddock and mix well but take care not to break up the fish too much. Use a cooking ring or your hands to form 4 fishcakes. Leave to one side until you're ready to serve.

For the sauce, finely chop the remaining half onion. Put 1 tbsp oil in a pan over a medium heat. When it's hot, add the onion and sweat for 5 minutes, taking care that it does not colour. Add the cream and cook for 3–4 minutes until it has reduced by half. Remove from the heat. Add the lemon juice, capers, shrimps and parsley. Season with salt and pepper.

To serve, heat a large non-stick frying pan over a medium heat. Add the remaining oil and when it's hot, add the fishcakes. Cook for 3–5 minutes, then turn and cook for 3–5 minutes more until golden brown on both sides. It's important not to turn the fishcakes too soon as they might break.

Gently reheat the sauce and divide it between the serving plates. For a starter, add 1 fishcake to each plate (or 2 for a main course). Garnish with watercress.

PORK FILLET IN A BERKSWELL CRUST WITH PAIMPOL BEAN AND BABY ARTICHOKE STEW

SERVES 4

4 tbsp olive oil
1 carrot, diced
1 small onion, diced
1 celery stick, diced
2 garlic cloves, chopped
300g (11oz) fresh paimpol beans
   or dried coco beans soaked
   overnight
1 bay leaf
1 sprig of rosemary, chopped
1 sprig of thyme, chopped
1 pork fillet
4 baby artichokes
1 plum tomato, deseeded
   and chopped
Salt and freshly ground
   black pepper
50g (1¾oz) Berkswell, shaved,
   to garnish

For the crust
100g (3½oz) white bread
100g (3½oz) Berkswell, grated
1 tbsp parsley
1 sage leaf
1 garlic clove
Grated zest of ¼ lemon
50g (1¾oz) unsalted butter

Berkswell is made in the county of Warwickshire in England using sheep's milk. It has a hard rind and a crumbly texture with sweet caramel and nutty flavours and a tangy finish.

Or look for a light, hard sheep's cheese with a fruity flavour.

For the crust, put the bread, Berkswell, parsley, sage, garlic, lemon zest and salt and pepper in a food processor. Blitz well, then add the butter and blitz again to make a smooth paste. Put the mixture between 2 sheets of cling film, then roll it out to a thickness of 5mm (¼in). Refrigerate for 1 hour until hard.

Meanwhile prepare the stew. Put 2 tbsp oil in a large pan over a medium heat. When it's hot, add the carrot, onion, celery and garlic. Reduce the heat and sweat for 5 minutes. Add the beans, bay leaf, rosemary and thyme. Cover with water to a depth of at least three fingers and bring to the boil. Reduce the heat and simmer for 30–35 minutes, until the beans are tender. Halfway through cooking, add salt to taste. Discard the bay leaf, drain the beans.

Next, start the pork. Preheat the oven to 200°C (400°F/Gas 6).

Cut the pork into 4 pieces and season. Put 1 tbsp oil in a pan over a medium heat, and when it's hot add the pork and sear for 3 minutes until golden brown.

Remove the crust from the fridge and cut it into 4 pieces, large enough to cover a piece of pork. Cover the pieces of pork in the crust, put on a baking tray and bake for 10–12 minutes until the crust is coloured but the pork is still juicy. If you have a meat thermometer, the interior of the pork should be 72°C (162°F).

Next, prepare the artichokes. Trim the stems and pull off the tough outer leaves. Spread the remaining leaves apart and pull out the innermost leaves to reveal the hairy choke. Scrape away the hairs using a teaspoon, then trim off the tops of the remaining leaves. Cut the hearts in half.

Put the remaining oil in a large pan over a medium heat. When it's hot, add the artichokes and season. Add the cooked beans and the chopped tomato. Reduce the heat and cook for 10 minutes until the artichokes are tender. Remove the pork from the oven and leave to rest for few minutes. Serve on top of the stew garnished with shavings of Berkswell.

TOMATO TARTE TATIN WITH SAINT NICOLAS DE LA DALMERIE

Tarte tatin is traditionally an apple-based dessert, but the same technique using tomato and mild goats' cheese makes an inventive savoury version.

Start by preheating the oven to 190°C (375°F/Gas 5) and butter two 15cm (6in) diameter tart tins.

Next, remove the tomato skins for a better tart. Score the skin of the tomatoes a couple of times. Put in a bowl of boiling water for few seconds, then in a bowl of iced water. Gently remove the skin.

Put the peeled tomatoes in a bowl with the sugar, vinegar and thyme. Drizzle with oil and season with salt and pepper. Arrange the tomatoes in the buttered tins.

Roll out the pastry and cut to fit the top of the tins. Prick with a fork and lay on top of the tomatoes. Bake for 20 minutes, or until the pastry is golden brown.

Remove from the oven and leave to cool for a few minutes, then place a serving plate on top of each tart. Turn the plate and tart over gently so the tart slips out on to the plate.

Crumble the Saint Nicolas de la Dalmerie on top of the tarts and flash under the grill for a few seconds.

Sprinkle with rocket and pine kernels.

SERVES 2

500g (1lb 2oz) (approx 20)
    heritage cherry tomatoes
    or regular cherry tomatoes
1 tbsp brown sugar
3 tbsp balsamic vinegar
½ tsp finely chopped thyme leaves
Olive oil, for drizzling
1 x 320g (11oz) sheet of chilled
    puff pastry
120g (scant 4½oz)
    Saint Nicolas de la Dalmerie
Handful of rocket
½ tbsp pine kernels
Salt and freshly ground
    black pepper

Saint Nicolas de la Dalmerie is made in the Languedoc-Roussillon region in South France using goats' milk. It's a mild cheese with hints of thyme and rosemary.

Or look for a firm goats' cheese with herby flavours and smooth texture.

TUNA NIÇOISE WITH A EWES' YOGURT DRESSING

SERVES 2

300g (11oz) fresh tuna loin
1 tbsp olive oil
1 tbsp chopped parsley
1 tbsp chopped chives
1 tbsp chopped chervil
100g (3½oz) new potatoes
100g (3½oz) French beans
2 quail eggs
6 cherry tomatoes
1 small red onion, finely sliced
6 black olives
6 caperberries
Salt and freshly ground
    black pepper

For the dressing
120g (scant 4½oz) ewes' yogurt
Juice of ½ lemon
1 tbsp olive oil

Here, the timeless salad from the sun-baked South of France gets an extra element from the yogurt dressing.

Prepare the fish first by seasoning the tuna with salt and pepper. Then heat the oil in a pan over a high heat. When hot, add the tuna and sear on all sides for 1 minute until golden brown but not cooked through.

Next, lay a piece of cling film on the work surface and sprinkle generously with the parsley, chives and chervil. Lay the seared tuna on top and rub with the herbs. Wrap the tuna tightly in the cling film and refrigerate while you prepare the rest of the dish.

Peel and cut the potatoes into quarters and put in a pan of cold, salted water. Bring to the boil, then reduce the heat and simmer for 8 minutes until tender. Drain and set aside.

Bring another pan of water to the boil. Top and tail the beans and add to the pan. Reduce the heat and simmer for 4 minutes until al dente. Drain and set aside.

Bring a third pan of water to the boil. Add the quail eggs to the pan, reduce the heat and simmer for 3 minutes. Drain and set aside.

For the dressing, put the yogurt in a bowl with the lemon juice and oil. Mix together thoroughly and add salt and pepper to taste.

Halve the tomatoes and mix with the potatoes, beans and red onion.

Remove the tuna from the fridge and remove the cling film. Using a sharp knife, cut into slices.

Peel the quail eggs and cut in half.

Place slices of tuna on top of the salad and sprinkle with a few olives and caperberries. Add the halved quail eggs and serve.

Ewes' yogurt is a creamy yogurt made from sheep's milk with a mild and floral flavour. It's best to buy it from a good fromagerie, as it will be free from additives and artificial flavourings.

CLAFOUTIS WITH PEACHES AND LA TUR

A classic clafoutis is made with cherries, but peaches work really well with the creamy La Tur.

Preheat the oven to 190°C (375°F/Gas 5). Butter 5 ramekins, each 10cm (4in) in diameter and 4cm (1½in) deep.

Whip the egg yolks with the caster sugar until fluffy. Then add the flour, milk, melted butter, grappa and salt to the yolk and sugar mixture. Mix together thoroughly.

In a separate bowl, beat the egg white until stiff.

Using a spatula, fold the beaten egg white into the flour mixture, slowly at first. Stir until the batter is smooth.

Three-quarters fill the prepared ramekins with the batter.

Slice the peaches into 1cm (½in) wedges. Cut the La Tur into ten 1cm (½in) slices.

Arrange wedges of peach and 2 slices of La Tur in a circle in each ramekin to cover the batter.

Sprinkle with thyme leaves and a little caster sugar.

Bake for 30–40 minutes until golden brown and risen.

Remove from the oven and dust with icing sugar. Leave to cool for a few minutes before serving.

SERVES 5

100g (3½oz) unsalted butter, melted, plus extra for greasing
3 egg yolks
80g (scant 3oz) caster sugar, plus extra for sprinkling
100g (3½oz) plain flour
200ml (7fl oz) full-fat milk
2 tbsp grappa or brandy
Pinch of salt
1 egg whit
2 peaches
1 La Tur
A few thyme leaves
1 tbsp icing sugar

La Tur is made in the Piemonte region of North Italy using a blend of cows', goats' and sheeps' milk. It's a rich, creamy cheese with a full, tangy flavour.

Or look for a smooth, spreadable, young soft cheese.

FIG AND RICOTTA TART
WITH RUM CUSTARD

There are few more welcome treats than an irresistibly ripe fig.

For the pastry, put the ground almonds, flour, butter, salt, egg yolks and sugar in a bowl and mix thoroughly to make a dough. Add 1 tbsp water if required to achieve a good consistency. Wrap in cling film and refrigerate for 1 hour.

Preheat the oven to 170°C (325°F/Gas 3). Remove the dough from the fridge and dust the work surface with flour. Roll the dough out to a thickness of 5mm and use to line a 20cm (8in) tart ring.

Prick the bottom with a fork, then cover the pastry with baking parchment and fill with ceramic baking beans or dried pulses. Bake blind for 20 minutes. Check that the pastry is cooked: the base should be dry and golden in colour. Cook for 5 minutes more if necessary.

Remove from the oven and leave to cool but do not turn the oven off.

Meanwhile, make the filling. Put the ricotta, egg yolks, sugar and lemon zest in a mixer and mix together thoroughly. Use the mixture to fill a piping bag fitted with a plain nozzle, then pipe the mixture over the surface of the pastry.

Cut each fig into 6 wedges and arrange on top of the filling, with a half fig in the centre.

Return the tart to the oven and bake for 10–15 minutes until the figs are tender.

Meanwhile make the rum custard. Mix the sugar and egg yolks together in a bowl. Bring the milk to the boil and when it starts to boil, add a little of the boiling milk to the sugar and egg yolk mixture to temper it. Then add all the sugar and egg yolk mixture to the boiling milk and cook slowly, stirring frequently until it thickens (do not allow to boil). Remove from the heat, add the rum and stir to combine.

Serve the tart with the rum custard alongside.

SERVES 8

8–10 black figs

For the pastry
225g (8oz) ground almonds
90g (scant 3½oz) plain flour, plus extra for dusting
125g (4½oz) unsalted butter
Pinch of salt
4 egg yolks
50g (1¾oz) caster sugar
1 tbsp water (optional)

For the filling
500g (1lb 2oz) ricotta
4 egg yolks
50g (1¾oz) caster sugar
Grated zest of 1 lemon

For the rum custard
35g (1oz) caster sugar
4 egg yolks
250ml (8fl oz) full-fat milk
1 tbsp rum

Ricotta is made in Italy: broadly using sheep's milk in the south of the country and cows' milk in the north.

Or look for A fresh, mild curd cheese with a sweet, earthy and slightly acidic flavour.

SUMMER CHEESEBOARD

Barkham Blue

A buttery and spicy blue cows' cheese made in Berkshire, England

Délice des Cabasses

A fresh sheep's curd cheese from the Midi-Pyrénées with a tangy, sweet flavour and refreshing finish (see p39)

Lou Sounal

A soft sheep's cheese from Lozère with a complex, earthy flavour

Beaufort d'Eté

A summer Beaufort (unlike Beaufort d'Alpage) from Savoy made from cows' milk with a mild, sweet flavour

Souréliette

A semi-hard sheep's milk from the Midi-Pyrénées with a bright, fruity, fresh-hazelnut flavour (see p46)

AUTUMN
CHEDDAR, GRUYÈRE AND THE SEMI-HARD CHEESES

Overleaf: A shelf topped with Bleu de Termignon – a rare, blue-veined cheese made in the Rhône-Alpes

As the seasons change and the weather gets cooler, there's more humidity and less light. The quality and flavour of the grass changes, which has a knock-on effect on the flavour of the milk and cheese.

In autumn, we start to see fewer fresh goats' cheeses, but this is also when the first mature cheeses made with spring milk start to appear – we finally can enjoy Tomme from the Alps. We always find that soft cheeses with bloomy rinds are amazing at the beginning of autumn too. In reality it's the end of their particular season, but the milk tends to be richer in taste as it matures over these months.

Autumn cheese feels less fresh on the tongue, but it also has a lot more character than younger cheeses, often a distinctly different flavour, with hints of mushrooms and flowers. It's the ideal time to eat medium-hard cheeses like Lincolnshire Poacher and West Country Farmhouse Cheddar: we serve it after it has been matured for 14 to 16 months. It's made with summer milk but at its most flavoursome in autumn of the following year.

That's the beauty and magic of this season – as the weather gets colder, the flavours get warmer. The combination of the fresh notes from spring milk with the stronger tastes and mushroomy character of mature cheese that we get in the colder months is what makes autumn a special time.

BAVETTES AU ROQUEFORT

SERVES 2

4 tbsp vegetable oil
80g (scant 3oz) unsalted butter
300g (11oz) shallots, finely sliced
300g (11oz) ratte potatoes
2 x 180g (scant 6½oz) beef
    bavettes or skirt steak
1 sprig of rosemary
2 garlic cloves, crushed
125ml (4½fl oz) dry red wine
200g (7oz) crème fraîche
100g (3½oz) Roquefort, crumbled
2 tbsp veal gravy or stock
1 tbsp chopped chives
Salt and freshly ground
    black pepper

Bavette or skirt steaks are an often forgotten cut, but their strong beefy flavour stands up admirably to creamy Roquefort.

Start by preparing an accompaniment of caramelised shallots. Put 1 tbsp oil and a knob of butter in a pan over a medium heat. When they are hot, add the shallots. Reduce the heat and sweat for 20 minutes, stirring frequently, until caramelised. Add a little water if the shallots start to stick.

Cut the potatoes in half and put in a pan of cold, salted water. Bring to the boil, then reduce the heat and simmer for 8 minutes until tender. Drain well.

Put a pan over a medium-high heat and when hot, add 2 tbsp oil. Add the cooked potatoes and sauté, stirring, for 10–15 minutes until golden.

Next, season the bavettes well with salt and pepper on both sides. Put a pan over a medium heat and when hot, add 1 tbsp oil. Add the bavettes and sear on both sides until golden brown all over. Add a knob of butter, then the rosemary and garlic.

When the butter starts to foam, spoon it around the bavettes. Reduce the heat and cook for 5 minutes on each side for rare cooking. Remove to a plate and cover with foil to keep warm.

To make a simple Roquefort sauce, remove the excess fat, the rosemary and the garlic from the pan. Add the wine to deglaze the pan, increase the heat and cook until the wine has reduced by half. Add the crème fraiche and the Roquefort, and stir until the cheese has melted. Add the veal gravy or stock, and the chives.

Just before serving, add a knob of butter to the potatoes and toss together over a low heat to warm through.

Divide the Roquefort sauce between the serving plates (or serve on the side), then add a bavette to each plate together with some shallots and potatoes.

Roquefort is made in the Midi-Pyrénées region of South France. Its creamy, fudgy texture is marked by greeny-blue veins.

Or look for a blue cheese with sweet, sharp and spicy flavours.

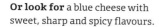

EMMENTAL, BRIE AND SERRANO HAM CROQUETTES

MAKES 24 CROQUETTES

85g (3oz) unsalted butter
325g (11½oz) plain flour
500ml (16fl oz) full-fat milk
Pinch of freshly grated nutmeg
100g (3½oz) Emmental, grated
50g (1¾oz) Brie de Meaux,
    crumbled
100g (3½oz) Serrano ham,
    finely chopped
6 eggs
2 tbsp water
1 litre (1¾ pints) sunflower oil
200g (7oz) panko breadcrumbs
Freshly ground black pepper

Start by making the cheesy croquette mixture. Put the butter in a pan over a medium heat. When melted, add 125g (4½oz) flour and stir with a whisk to make a roux. Cook, stirring continuously, for about 1 minute, or until the flour is cooked.

Add the milk in parts and continue stirring. Reduce the heat and stir until the mixture thickens. Add the nutmeg and black pepper to taste. Then add the Emmental, Brie and Serrano ham. Mix well to a smooth consistency.

Place the mixture in a bowl, leave to cool, then refrigerate until cold.

Beat the eggs in a bowl with the water. Set aside ready to breadcrumb your croquettes.

Heat the oil in a pan to 170°C (325°F).

Meanwhile, remove the cheese and ham mixture from the fridge and put in a piping bag fitted with a plain nozzle.

Pipe the mixture into croquette-shaped logs, about 2cm (¾in) in diameter and 10cm (4in) long.

Very gently dip the croquettes in the remaining flour, then in the beaten egg mixture, then in the breadcrumbs. Finally, dip again in the egg, then in the breadcrumbs.

Fry the croquettes in 2 batches in the hot oil until golden brown. When ready, remove to kitchen paper to drain. Serve hot.

Emmental is best known as a Swiss cheese but is also made in the Rhône-Alpes region of South-West France. Here, it has a mild, slightly lactic flavour.

Or look for a pasteurised cows' milk cheese with a buttery, nutty flavour that's good for melting.

MONTGOMERY CHEDDAR AND PALE ALE RAREBIT WITH CAULIFLOWER

SERVES 6

50g (1¾oz) unsalted butter
50g (1¾oz) plain flour
165ml (6fl oz) pale ale
165g (scant 6oz) Montgomery
    Cheddar, grated
3 tsp balsamic vinegar
6 tsp Worcestershire sauce
1 heaped tbsp wholegrain mustard
1 egg yolk
150g (5½oz) cauliflower, cut into
    small florets
600g (1lb 5oz) pain de campagne
2 tbsp chopped parsley, to garnish

This is the best Welsh rarebit you'll ever eat – the cauliflower and pale ale make it extra thick and velvety.

To make the Welsh rarebit mixture, put the butter in a pan over a medium heat. When the butter has melted, add the flour. Stir with a whisk to make a roux. Cook, stirring continuously, for about 1 minute, or until the flour is cooked, then add the pale ale in parts and continue stirring.

When the mixture starts to thicken, add the Montgomery Cheddar, vinegar, Worcestershire sauce and mustard. Stir until it's all smooth, remove from the heat, then add the egg yolk.

Put the cauliflower in a pan of boiling salted water and cook for 2 minutes so it retains some crunch. Drain well, then add to the Welsh rarebit mix.

Preheat the grill. Cut the bread into 6 thick slices and place under the grill to toast on both sides.

Spread the Welsh rarebit mix on top of each slice of toast and return to the grill. Grill for 5–8 minutes until the rarebit is golden brown and bubbling.

Sprinkle with parsley and serve.

Montgomery Cheddar is made in the county of Somerset in South-West England mainly using the milk of Friesian cows. It has a firm texture and caramel sweetness.

Or look for a fruity, nutty and sweet cows' cheese.

RACLETTE AND EMMENTAL CROQUE-MONSIEUR WITH TRUFFLE OIL

Go the extra mile for this inventive take on a croque-monsieur and you won't regret it – it's the ultimate version of the cheesy French icon.

To make the cheese topping, put the milk and cornflour in a pan over a low heat. Stir continuously with a whisk, cooking slowly until the mixture thickens. Add the Raclette and 200g (7oz) Emmental. Stir with a spatula until the cheeses have melted. Stir in the truffle oil, truffle paste and egg yolk.

Line a baking tray with a double layer of cling film. Pour over the cheese and refrigerate for 30 minutes until firm.

Meanwhile, preheat the grill.

Cut the hardened cheese topping into 6 pieces, each a little larger than a slice of the pain de mie (or sandwich bread).

Put 12 slices of bread under the grill until lightly toasted on both sides.

Divide the ham between 6 of the slices and top with the remaining Emmental. Replace under the grill and when the cheese has melted, top with the remaining 6 slices of toast.

Finally, top each croque-monsieur with a slice of cheese topping and return to the grill until brown and bubbling.

Serve with chips to make a complete meal.

SERVES 6

100ml (3½fl oz) full-fat milk
1 heaped tbsp cornflour
200g (7oz) Raclette, grated
450g (1lb) Emmental, grated
½ tbsp truffle oil
½ tbsp black truffle paste
1 egg yolk
12 slices of pain de mie (or sandwich bread)
600g (1lb 5oz) cooked ham

Raclette is made in the Rhône-Alpes region of West France using cows' milk. It's a semi-hard cheese that's ideal for melting.

Or look for a creamy, semi-hard cows' cheese with a rich, pronounced flavour.

EINKORN, WESTCOMBE CHEDDAR AND CONFIT ONION BREAD

Einkorn is an ancient form of wheat with a distinctive flavour.

Make the bread mix first by putting the flour and salt in a large bowl.

Then put the yeast and sugar in a small bowl with 100ml (3½fl oz) warm water. Stir to dissolve.

Add the yeast mixture and the remaining warm water to the flour and salt mixture. Work together with your fingertips until the ingredients are well incorporated but the mixture is still a little wet. Take care not to overwork the mixture.

Cover with a clean tea towel and leave to prove at room temperature for 3–4 hours, depending on the temperature of the room, until the dough has doubled in size.

Meanwhile, make the onion confit. Put the onion in a pan with the wine and butter over a low heat. Bring to the boil, then reduce the heat and simmer until the wine has evaporated and the onion is translucent. Season with a pinch of salt and pepper and set aside.

Butter a 20cm (8in) loaf tin and dust with flour.

Stir the onion confit and Westcombe Cheddar into the bread mixture and mix well to incorporate all the ingredients. Form into a loaf shape and place in the prepared tin.

Cover with a clean tea towel and leave to prove at room temperature for a further 1–2 hours, or until the dough has almost reached the top of the tin.

Preheat the oven to 200°C (400°F/Gas 6) and then bake the loaf for 30 minutes, then reduce the temperature to 180°C (350°F/Gas 4) for a further 30 minutes until a toothpick emerges clean from the loaf.

Remove from the oven and leave to cool.

Serve with piccalilli and Cheddar cheese.

MAKES 1 X 20CM (8IN) LOAF

500g (1lb 2oz) Einkorn flour, plus extra for dusting
1 tbsp salt
7g (1 heaped tsp) dried active yeast
½ tbsp caster sugar
350ml (scant 12fl oz) warm water
200g (7oz) onion, finely chopped
200ml (7fl oz) dry white wine
50g (1¾oz) unsalted butter, plus extra for greasing
200g (7oz) Westcombe Cheddar, grated
Salt and freshly ground black pepper
Piccalilli, to serve
Cheddar cheese, to serve

Westcombe Cheddar is made in the county of Somerset in South West England. It's a hard cheese with citrus, hazelnut and caramel flavours.

Or look for a semi-hard, cows' milk cheese with a slightly tangy finish.

GALETTES BRETONNES WITH WILD MUSHROOMS AND GRUYÈRE

For the galette batter, put the buckwheat flour, plain flour, butter, egg, milk and water in a bowl. Whisk together thoroughly then refrigerate for 30 minutes.

Meanwhile, cut the mushrooms into chunks. Put 2 tbsp oil in a large frying pan over a high heat. Add the mushrooms and sauté for 5 minutes until lightly browned, then season with salt and pepper. Reduce the heat and add a knob of butter and the shallot. Stir well and cook for a few minutes until the shallot is translucent. Add the wine, increase the heat and cook for 2–3 minutes until the alcohol has evaporated. Set aside.

Put 50g (1¾oz) butter in another pan over a medium heat. When it's hot, add the leek and cook for 8 minutes until soft but not coloured. Add the softened leek to the pan with the mushrooms and allow to cool a little. Then add half the Gruyère, the parsley and the thyme. Mix well and set aside.

Too cook the galettes, put 1 tbsp oil in a 20cm (8in) non-stick pan over a medium heat. When it's hot, ladle in enough batter to coat the pan thinly. Cook for a few minutes until the mixture is firm, then turn the galette over and cook the other side for 1 minute. Repeat until all the batter is used up; you may have to add more oil. Remove each cooked galette to a plate.

Preheat the oven to 190°C (375°F/Gas 5).

In the centre of each galettes, place a generous spoonful of mushroom mixture and fold the galette up. Arrange the filled galettes in a buttered baking tray and bake for 10 minutes until brown and crispy outside.

Meanwhile, make the cheese sauce. Put the cream in a pan over a medium heat and bring to boil. Reduce the heat and simmer for 5 minutes until the cream has reduced slightly. Remove from the heat and add the remaining Gruyère. Stir well and when the cheese has melted, add the egg yolks. Whisk thoroughly to make a smooth sauce then season with nutmeg, salt and pepper. Serve the sauce alongside the galettes.

SERVES 6

800g (1¾lb) mixed wild mushrooms (for example, girolles, pied de mouton, chanterelles, cèpes)
5–6 tbsp vegetable oil
80g (scant 3oz) unsalted butter
1 shallot, finely chopped
125ml (4½fl oz) dry white wine
1 leek, thinly sliced
400g (14oz) Gruyère, coarsely grated
1 tbsp finely chopped parsley
1 tbsp finely chopped thyme leaves
500ml (16fl oz) double cream
2 egg yolks
2–3 gratings of nutmeg
Salt and freshly ground black pepper

For the batter
250g (9½oz) buckwheat flour
20g (¾oz) plain flour
30g (1oz) unsalted butter, melted
1 egg
250ml (8fl oz) full-fat milk
250ml (8fl oz) water

Gruyère is made in the region of the same name in West Switzerland using cows' milk. It's a firm cheese with a salty flavour that becomes more earthy and complex with age.

Or look for a hard, pasteurised cows' cheese with a pronounced flavour.

PARMESAN, CARDAMOM AND SPICY LINCOLNSHIRE POACHER CRISPS

400g (14oz) Parmesan,
   aged 24 months and finely
   grated
Pinch of ground cardamom
Freshly ground black pepper
400g (14oz) Lincolnshire Poacher,
   finely grated
2 pinches of paprika
2 pinches of cayenne pepper

These easy-to-make crisps go down a storm in the Androuet restaurant. A perfect nibble with a good wine or beer.

Put a non-stick pan over a high heat and when it's hot, sprinkle over the Parmesan in a thin layer to make a rough circle. You can use a cooking ring to form the circle if you prefer.

As soon as the cheese starts to melt and become golden brown, sprinkle with a little cardamom and some black pepper.

Using a spatula, remove the Parmesan crisp from the pan and place on a rolling pin so the crisp becomes slightly curved. Leave to cool then remove to a plate. Repeat with the remaining Parmesan.

Repeat the whole process using the Lincolnshire Poacher, this time sprinkling the melting cheese with paprika and cayenne pepper.

Lincolnshire Poacher is made in the West Midlands in England using cows' milk. It's a hard cheese with an intense, almost meaty flavour.

Or look for a raw, hard, pressed cows' cheese with a strong and rich flavour.

PORK BELLY WITH SWEET POTATO MASH, RAINBOW KALE AND AGED PECORINO SARDO

For a tender, juicy meat, the pork needs to brine overnight, so start the day before the dish is to be served. To make the brine, put the water, salt, carrot, onion and celery in a large pan over a medium heat. Bring to the boil, then remove from the heat and add the bay leaves, thyme, peppercorns and coriander seeds. Leave to cool.

Place the pork belly in a non-reactive container (plastic, glass or stainless steel), pour over the prepared cold brine and 200ml (7fl oz) wine. Refrigerate overnight, covered with cling film.

The next day, preheat the oven to 200°C (400°F/Gas 6).

Remove the pork belly from the brine and pat it dry with kitchen paper. Score the skin several times with the tip of a sharp knife, rub in the oil and sprinkle with salt. Place in a roasting tin and cook for 30 minutes. Reduce the heat to 160°C (325°F/Gas 3), cook for 2–3 hours more, until the meat is tender.

Meanwhile, make the mash. Peel and cut the potatoes and the sweet potatoes into chunks. Put in a pan of cold, salted water. Bring to the boil, then reduce the heat and simmer for 15 minutes. Drain thoroughly. Add the butter, stir well, then crush with a fork. Add the Pecorino, rosemary and chives, and season.

To prepare the kale, trim its tough outer leaves and the tough stems from the kale then add to a pan of boiling salted water and cook for 5 minutes. Drain and set aside. Put 50g (1¾oz) butter in a frying pan over a medium heat. When the butter starts to foam, add the garlic and drained kale. Stir to combine, then sauté for a few minutes.

When the pork is ready, leave it in the oven and turn on the oven grill. Grill until the skin is crispy, then remove from the oven and leave to rest for 5 minutes. Meanwhile, add the remaining wine to the roasting tin and put over a medium heat to deglaze the tin. Strain the pan juices through a fine sieve.

Carve the pork, divide the mash and kale between the plates, drizzle with the pan juices and garnish with shaved Pecorino.

SERVES 6

800ml (28fl oz) water
30g (1oz) salt
1 carrot, peeled and cut into chunks
1 onion, cut into chunks
1 celery stick, cut into chunks
3 bay leaves
2 sprigs of thyme
1 tbsp black peppercorns
1 tbsp coriander seeds
1.5kg (3lb 3oz) boneless pork belly
400ml (14fl oz) dry white wine
5 tbsp vegetable oil
300g (11oz) rainbow kale
50g (1¾oz) unsalted butter
1 garlic clove, crushed
Rock salt and freshly ground black pepper
80g (scant 3oz) aged Pecorino Sardo, shaved, to serve

For the mash
300g (11oz) desiree potatoes
600g (1lb 5oz) sweet potatoes
50g (1¾oz) unsalted butter
100g (3½oz) aged Pecorino Sardo, grated
1 tsp chopped rosemary
1 tbsp chopped chives

Pecorino Sardo is made on the Italian island of Sardinia using sheep's milk. It's a semi-hard creamy cheese with a fruity, fresh and earthy flavour.

Or look for a semi-hard, sheep's cheese with sweet, slightly acidic character.

POULET DE BRESSE WITH POTATO, CELERIAC AND PARSNIP MASH AND MORBIER SAUCE

SERVES 4

1 poulet de Bresse
1 bay leaf
200g (7oz) carrots, diced, trimmings reserved
3 celery stalks, diced, trimmings reserved
1 onion, diced, trimmings reserved
Plain flour, for dusting
4 tbsp vegetable oil
50g (1¾oz) unsalted butter
4 garlic cloves, finely chopped
1 heaped tbsp finely chopped thyme
300g (11oz) mixed wild mushrooms (for example, girolles, pied de mouton, chanterelles, cèpes)
400ml (14fl oz) dry sherry
200g (7oz) crème fraîche
150g (5½oz) Morbier, grated
Salt and freshly ground black pepper
1 tbsp chopped tarragon, to serve

For the mash
200g (7oz) desiree potatoes
200g (7oz) celeriac
200g (7oz) parsnips
Knob of unsalted butter

Morbier is made in the Franche-Comté region of West France using cows' milk. It has a soft, smooth texture and a lightly creamy, fruity flavour with vegetable charcoal running dramatically through its centre.

Or look for a semi-hard cows' cheese with fruity character.

Start with the stock. Cut the poulet de Bresse into 8 pieces and remove the breastbone. You can ask your butcher to do this. Rinse the bones and put in a pan with the bay leaf and the trimmings from the carrots, celery and onion. Cover with cold water, bring to the boil and simmer for 1 hour. Strain through a sieve and set aside.

Meanwhile, season the chicken pieces with salt and pepper. Dust with flour. Put the oil in a cast-iron casserole dish over a medium heat until hot. Add the chicken and fry for 10 minutes until golden brown all over. Remove from the pan and set aside.

Drain the fat from the casserole dish, return the dish to the heat and add the butter. Add the carrots, celery, onion, garlic and thyme. Sweat for 5 minutes until brown.

Meanwhile, clean the mushrooms and cut into chunks. Add to the vegetables and season with salt and pepper.

Preheat the oven to 180°C (350°F/Gas 4).

Return the chicken to the casserole dish and add the sherry. Increase the heat and cook for a few minutes until the alcohol has evaporated. Add the prepared stock, cover the casserole dish and cook in the oven for 1½ hours.

To make the mash, peel and cut the potatoes, celeriac and parsnips into chunks and put in a pan of cold, salted water. Bring to the boil, then reduce the heat and simmer for 15 minutes until tender. Drain and put in a pan with the butter. Mash well and season. Cover with a lid to keep warm.

Take the casserole dish from the oven and remove the chicken and mushrooms to a serving dish with a slotted spoon. If the sauce is too thin, put the casserole dish on the hob over a medium heat until the sauce has thickened. Add the crème fraîche and Morbier and stir well to combine.

Serve the chicken, mushrooms and mash topped with the sauce and a sprinkle of tarragon.

ROAST BUTTERNUT SQUASH WITH VINTAGE GOUDA

This attractive dish can be a light main course, or an unusual accompaniment to roast pork or lamb.

For the dressing, mix together the vegetable oil, hazelnut oil, vinegar, shallot and mustard. Season with salt and pepper and refrigerate while you prepare the rest of the dish.

Preheat the oven to 180°C (350°F/Gas 4).

Peel the squash and cut into long, narrow chunks. Put on a baking tray and add the honey, thyme and garlic. Drizzle with oil and season with salt and pepper.

Bake for 30 minutes, or until tender. Set aside to cool.

Put the frisée lettuce and cooked, cooled squash in a large bowl. Cut half the Gouda into cubes and add to the bowl. Toss with half the dressing.

Shave the cèpe and the remaining Gouda over the top. Sprinkle with the pumpkin seeds and chives. Drizzle with the remaining dressing and serve.

SERVES 4

1 butternut squash
2 tbsp clear honey
1 tsp chopped thyme leaves
1 garlic clove, crushed
Olive oil, for drizzling
1 head of frisée lettuce,
    torn into small pieces
200g (7oz) vintage Gouda
1 fresh cèpe, trimmed and cleaned
1 tbsp pumpkin seeds, toasted
½ tbsp chopped chives
Salt and freshly ground
    black pepper

For the dressing
4 tbsp vegetable oil
2 tbsp hazelnut oil
2 tbsp cider vinegar
1 small shallot, chopped
½ tsp Dijon mustard

Gouda is made in Holland using cows' milk. Its character changes considerably as it ages. Aged Gouda is hard with flavours of dried fruits and toasted seeds.

Or look for a mature Gouda or a rich, hard cows' cheese.

VEAL PAUPIETTES WITH MORELS AND TOMME DE MONTAGNE

SERVES 4

30g (1oz) morels
1 tbsp unsalted butter
1 shallot, chopped
2 garlic cloves, chopped
4 veal escalopes
2 slices of white bread
100ml (3½fl oz) full-fat milk
60g (2oz) Tomme de Montagne,
   grated
1 tbsp chopped parsley
1 carrot, diced
1 celery stick, diced
1 onion, diced
2 sprigs of thyme, leaves only
4 plum tomatoes or 1 x 200g (7oz)
   can chopped tomatoes in juice
200ml (7fl oz) dry white wine
Salt and freshly ground
   black pepper
Tarragon leaves, to garnish

Tomme de Montagne is made in the Rhône-Alpes region in France using cows' milk. It's matured longer than most Tommes and its character can vary depending on the producer.

Or look for a semi-hard, cows' cheese with a delicate flavour.

The morels, veal trimmings, bread and Tomme de Montagne create the filling mixture for these veal paupiettes.

Start by preparing the morels. Clean and roughly chop the morels. Put the butter in a pan over a medium heat until hot. Add the morels, shallot and half the garlic. Reduce the heat and sweat for 5 minutes. Season with salt and pepper, then discard the garlic. Place the morel mixture in a bowl and set aside.

Beat the veal escalopes with a rolling pin to flatten them to a thickness of about 5mm (¼in). Trim to make 4 squares, leaving the remaining trimmings to one side.

Put the bread in a small bowl with the milk to soak. Put the offcuts of veal in a food processor. Squeeze out the bread, add to the veal offcuts, and blend to a smooth paste. Put in a bowl and add the cooked morels, the Tomme de Montagne and the parsley. Season with salt and pepper.

Divide the mixture between the escalopes, placing it in the centre of each. Fold the escalopes to enclose the mixture and tie with string to create the paupiettes. Season with salt and pepper.

Put 2 tbsp oil in a pan over a high heat. When it is hot, add the veal paupiettes and fry for 8 minutes, stirring occasionally, until golden brown all over.

Add the carrot, celery, onion, remaining garlic and the thyme to the pan with the paupiettes. Cook, stirring, for a few minutes more until the vegetables are slightly coloured.

If using fresh tomatoes, remove their skins for a smoother sauce. Score the skin, put in a bowl of boiling water for few seconds, then in a bowl of iced water. Remove the skin and seeds, then chop the flesh. Add the tomatoes and wine to the pan. If using canned tomatoes, also add the juice.

Cover with a lid, reduce the heat and cook for about ½ hour until the meat is tender. Serve sprinkled with tarragon.

BOURDALOUE TART WITH WHIPPED PETIT SUISSE

The addition of Petit Suisse may seem inconsequential, but just a small spoonful of it totally transforms this sweet French staple.

For the pastry, put the flour and sugar in a bowl and make a well in the centre. Add the butter and rub it into the flour and sugar using your fingertips until the mixture resembles coarse breadcrumbs. Add the beaten egg and blend to make a smooth, soft dough. Wrap in cling film and refrigerate for 30 minutes.

Preheat the oven to 170°C (325°F/Gas 3).

Roll out the pastry on a lightly floured surface to make a 40cm (16in) diameter circle about 5mm (¼in) thick.

Use the pastry to line a 30cm (12in) diameter tart ring and prick the bottom with a fork. Cover the pastry with baking parchment and fill with ceramic baking beans or dried pulses.

Bake blind for 20 minutes. Remove from the oven and remove the baking parchment and beans. Leave to cool slightly, but leave the oven on.

Meanwhile, make the frangipane filling. Beat together the sugar and butter until pale in colour. Beat in the eggs, then the ground almonds.

Fill a piping bag fitted with a plain nozzle with the mixture and pipe over the half-cooked pastry base.

Increase the oven temperature to 180°C (350°F/Gas 4).

Core and thinly slice the pears, then arrange on top of the frangipane.

Put the apricot jam in a pan over a medium heat with 1 tbsp water. Use this mixture to brush the top of the tart. Bake for 25 minutes until golden brown. Leave to cool before cutting.

Meanwhile, lightly whip together the Petit Suisse and the vanilla essence. Serve with the warm tart.

SERVES 8

200g (7oz) caster sugar
200g (7oz) unsalted butter
2 eggs
200g (7oz) ground almonds
3 pears
2 tbsp apricot jam
200g (7oz) Petit Suisse
½ tbsp vanilla essence

For the pastry
225g (8oz) plain flour, plus extra for dusting
80g (scant 3oz) caster sugar
110g (scant 4oz) unsalted butter, cut into small cubes
1 egg, beaten

Petit Suisse is a French fresh curd cheese made with cows' milk and cream. It has a thick, yogurt-like texture and delicate, creamy flavour.

Or look for a curd cheese with a subtle flavour that can be spooned.

AUTUMN
CHEESEBOARD

Bleu du Val d'Aillons
A blue-veined cows' cheese from Savoy with a melting, creamy texture

Brillat-Savarin
A triple cream cows' milk cheese from Île-de-France or Burgundy with a rich hint of crème fraiche (see p35, p60)

Salers
A hard, buttery cows' cheese from Auvergne with complex grassy, peppery and citrus flavours

Soumaintrain
A soft cows' cheese from Burgundy washed in white wine for a mild, fruity and creamy flavour

Aarewasser
A medium-hard Swiss cows' cheese from Oberhünigen with a mild, earthy flavour and creamy texture

WINTER
REBLOCHON, COMTÉ AND THE BOLD CHEESES

Overleaf: A beautiful round of Tomme Fermiere cows' milk cheese maturing on site at the producer's farm

Winter is all about bold character. For thousands of years, people traditionally started producing and storing their cheeses in summer in preparation for the colder months ahead. That hasn't changed: winter means big, strong flavours.

Fresh cheeses may all have but disappeared by the time you get to January and February, but that doesn't mean winter is any less exciting. There's lots of incredibly creamy Beaufort (which just melts in your mouth) and medium-hard Swiss cheeses such as Aarewasser and Vacherin Fribourgeois, which have been aged for six months using spring and summer milks.

Winter is also the traditional season for Mont d'Or. When the animals milked for Comté cheese are moved from the mountains down to the valleys for winter (away from the cold), they have less verdant grass to graze on. So instead of Comté (which requires a higher-quality milk), the farmers produce Mont d'Or – a beautiful soft cheese packaged in spruce for a wonderful, delicate flavour.

And we can't talk about winter without mentioning the beautiful blue Stilton: the king of English cheeses. It's at its best from December to April, because its milk is actually produced in summer but it needs at least two to three months to reach its optimum taste.

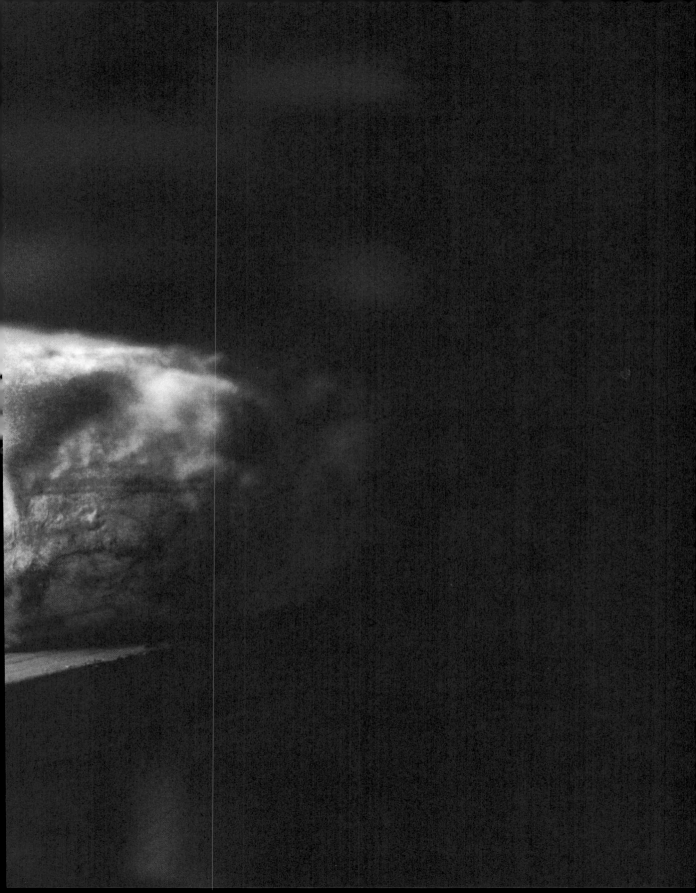

BAKED CAMEMBERT WITH ROSEMARY, HONEY AND ALMONDS

This cold-weather favourite is easy to make but always popular.

To prepare it, preheat the oven to 190°C (375°F/Gas 5).

Remove the cheese from its packaging and place in a Camembert dish. If you do not have a Camembert dish, cut a circle of baking parchment 2cm (¾in) larger in diameter than the cheese. Wet the parchment under cold water and lie it in the Camembert box. Replace the cheese in its parchment-lined box.

Using a sharp knife, score the top of the Camembert in a criss-cross pattern. Put the sprigs of rosemary in the cuts and drizzle with honey.

Bake for 10 minutes until the cheese is melting and the honey is starting to caramelise.

Meanwhile, cut the pear into chunks.

Carefully remove the Camembert from the oven and sprinkle with the flaked almonds.

Serve immediately, with the pieces of pear to dip into the melting Camembert.

SERVES 2

1 Camembert
4–5 small sprigs of rosemary
1 tbsp clear honey
1 pear
2 tbsp flaked and toasted almonds

Camembert is made in the Normandy region of North West France using cows' milk. It has a bloomy white rind and a soft, fragrant centre with a fruity and strong flavour.

Or look for a soft, melting cows' cheese with an earthy and rich flavour.

MONT D'OR VACHERIN MELT

SERVES 2

400g (14oz) new potatoes
1 garlic clove
1.5kg (3lb 3oz) Mont d'Or Vacherin
100ml (3½fl oz) dry white wine
Selection of charcuterie and
   cornichons, to serve

Much like Camembert, Mont d'Or Vacherin is an amazing cheese to bake. It's slightly pricier than Camembert and only available in the winter months, so it's an extra-special treat.

To prepare, preheat the oven to 190°C (375°F/Gas 5).

Put the unpeeled, whole potatoes in a pan with salt and cold water to cover. Bring to the boil, then reduce the heat and simmer for 10 minutes, or until tender.

Meanwhile, finely chop the garlic. Using a sharp knife, score the top of the cheese and remove it in one piece. Pour in the wine, followed by the garlic on to the remaining cheese. Gently stir the wine and garlic, then replace the top of the cheese.

Bake for 15–20 minutes until the cheese is hot but not overmelted.

Serve immediately with the boiled potatoes, which you can dip into the melted cheese, and with a selection of charcuterie and cornichons.

Mont d'Or Vacherin is made in the Jura region of Switzerland (in the French part of Jura it is called Vacherin du Haut-Doubs). It is rich, creamy and slightly sweet, and packed in a circular spruce box.

Or look for a melting cows' cheese with a washed rind and a deep flavour.

BEEF CHEEKS WITH GRUYÈRE ETIVAZ AND HORSERADISH MASH

It's best to marinate the beef overnight, so start the day before you want to serve. Mix together the wine, carrot, celery, onion, garlic, rosemary, thyme and bay leaf. Put the beef cheeks in a large, shallow dish, add the marinade and place in the fridge overnight. The next day, drain the beef cheeks, reserving the wine and vegetables (discard the herbs). Pat dry with kitchen paper.

Put 2 tbsp oil in a large pan over a medium heat. When hot, add the reserved vegetables and a pinch of salt. Sweat for a few minutes until golden brown.

Season the beef cheeks with salt and pepper and dust with flour. Put the remaining oil in another pan over a medium heat until hot, add the beef cheeks and sear them all over. Remove with a slotted spoon and add to the pan with the vegetables.

To remove the tomato skins for the sauce, score the skins, put in a bowl of boiling water for few seconds, then in a bowl of iced water. Remove the skin and seeds, then chop. Add the chopped tomatoes to the pan with the beef cheeks and vegetables. Add the wine from the marinade and bring to the boil. Add the stock, bring to the boil again, then reduce the heat. Cover the pan and simmer for about 2 hours, or until the meat is tender. If the cooking liquid becomes too thick, add water.

Meanwhile make the mashed potato. Peel and cut the potatoes in half and put in a pan with cold, salted water. Bring to the boil, then reduce the heat and simmer until tender. Drain then pass through a sieve or potato ricer.

Put the butter and milk in a large pan over a medium heat with the nutmeg. Bring to the boil, then add the mashed potato. Mix, then add horseradish to taste and the Gruyère Etivaz and mix.

When the beef cheeks are cooked, remove and slice thickly. Season the cooking sauce with salt and pepper.

Serve the beef cheek with the mashed potato and pour over the sauce, finish with some parsley and a little grated horseradish.

SERVES 6

750ml (1¼ pints) dry red wine
1 carrot, diced
1 celery stalk, diced
1 onion, diced
1 garlic clove, roughly chopped
1 sprig of rosemary, roughly chopped
1 sprig of thyme, roughly chopped
1 bay leaf
3 beef cheeks
4 tbsp vegetable oil
Plain flour, for dusting
2 plum tomatoes
400ml (14fl oz) beef stock
500g (1lb 2oz) desiree potatoes
50g (1¾oz) unsalted butter
100ml (3½fl oz) full-fat milk
Small grating of fresh nutmeg
1 tbsp fresh horseradish root, grated
100g (3½oz) Gruyère Etivaz, grated
Salt and freshly ground black pepper
Chopped parsley, to serve

Gruyère Etivaz is made in the Pays-d'Enhaut region of Switzerland using cows' milk. It is a hard Alpine cheese with a salty, mildly nutty flavour.

Or look for a hard, long-matured cows' cheese with an aromatic, fruity character.

DUCK BREAST WITH SARLADAISE POTATOES AND BLEU DES CAUSSES TURNIP TOPS

SERVES 4

500g (1lb 2oz) King Edward
  potatoes
1 tsp finely chopped thyme
200g (7oz) duck fat
2 garlic cloves, finely chopped
1 litre (1¾ pints) water
30g (1oz) salt
Grated zest of 1 orange
1 tbsp black peppercorns
1 tbsp coriander seeds
4 duck breasts
50g (1¾oz) unsalted butter
Salt and freshly ground
  black pepper

For the sauce
2 tbsp vegetable oil
1 carrot, cut in chunks
1 onion, cut into chunks
1 celery stick, cut into chunks
1 garlic clove, crushed
1 sprig of rosemary
1 sprig of thyme
3 tbsp balsamic vinegar
100ml (3½fl oz) dry red wine
500ml (16fl oz) chicken stock

For the turnip tops
500g (1lb 2oz) turnip tops
  (cime di rapa)
2 tbsp olive oil
1 shallot, finely chopped
160g (5½oz) Bleu des Causses,
  crumbled

For authentic sarladaise potatoes (cooked in duck fat), you need to prepare them the day before you want to serve. You'll also need to start the duck several hours before dishing up.

Preheat the oven to 160°C (325°F/Gas 3) and line a 15cm (6in) square ovenproof dish with parchment paper.

Peel the potatoes and use a mandolin to cut them into 2–3mm (1/12–1/8in) slices. Do not wash the slices.

Season with half the thyme and with salt and pepper. Toss well and set aside.

Put the duck fat, garlic and remaining thyme in a pan over a low heat. When the fat has melted, put 2 tbsp in the ovenproof dish and cover with some of the sliced potato to make a flat patty. Add more duck fat followed by more potato until all the fat and potato have been used up in the layers. Do not worry if there appears to be a lot of fat.

Bake for 30–40 minutes until the potatoes are soft. Remove from the oven and place another 15cm (6in) square ovenproof dish on top. Put a heavy weight on top of the second dish. Leave to cool then refrigerate overnight.

The next day, carefully scrape off any excess fat from the surface of the potatoes and cut into broad fingers. Set aside ready to warm through before serving.

Prepare the brine for the duck breasts. Put the water and salt in a pan over a medium heat and bring to the boil. Add the orange zest, peppercorns and coriander seeds, then remove from the heat and leave to cool.

When the brine is cold, put the duck breasts in a large shallow dish, cover with brine and refrigerate for 4 hours.

Continued overleaf

Meanwhile prepare the sauce. Put the vegetable oil in a pan over a medium heat. When it's hot, add the carrot, onion, celery and garlic. Cook, stirring, for 5 minutes, until the vegetables are browned all over, then add the rosemary, thyme, vinegar and wine. Increase the heat and cook for 10–15 minutes until the liquid has almost completely evaporated.

Add the stock and cook until the sauce has a syrupy consistency. Strain through a sieve into a pan and set aside.

Preheat the oven to 190°C (375°F/Gas 5).

Remove the duck breasts from the brine and pat dry with kitchen paper. Score the skin several times with a sharp knife.

Put the breasts in a cold frying pan, skin side down, over a medium heat. Cook for 5 minutes, or until the skin is golden and crispy, then turn the breasts over and sear the other side for about 5 minutes for medium-rare cooking.

Add the butter to the pan and when it has melted, use to baste the breasts. Remove from the heat, cover with foil and leave to rest for 10 minutes.

Meanwhile, put the fingers of potato on a baking sheet and warm through for 10 minutes. Put the sauce over a low heat and reheat gently.

Bring a pan of salted water to the boil, add the turnip tops, reduce the heat and cook for 3 minutes. The turnip tops should still be crunchy. Drain well and set aside.

Finish the turnip tops. Put the olive oil in a pan over a medium heat. When hot, reduce the heat, add the shallot and sauté gently for 1 minute until soft and translucent. Add the drained turnip tops and stir well to combine. Finally add the crumbled Bleu des Causses.

Slice the duck breasts and divide between the serving plates Add some sarladaise potato and some sautéed turnip tops. Drizzle with sauce and serve.

Bleu des Causses is made in the Midi-Pyrénées region of South France from cows' milk. It is firm and supple with open blue veins and a full-bodied taste.

Or look for a blue cows' cheese with a firm texture and a strong flavour.

MORTEAU SAUSAGE WITH TOMME DE LAGUIOLE ALIGOT

SERVES 2

1 Morteau sausage or other
  smoked sausage
20g (¾oz) wholegrain mustard

For the aligot
200g (7oz) desiree potatoes
Knob of unsalted butter
1 garlic clove, finely chopped
2 tbsp double cream
2 tbsp full-fat milk
200g (7oz) Tomme de Laguiole,
  grated
Salt and freshly ground
  black pepper
Grating of nutmeg

Tomme de Laguiole is made in
the Midi-Pyrénées region of South
France from cows' milk. It has a
sharp and slightly sour flavour.

Or look for a smooth, clean,
tangy cows' cheese.

Comfort food at its most comforting: smoky sausage,
potatoes, melted cheese and mustardy cream.

Start by making the aligot. Put the whole potatoes into a
pan of cold, salted water. Bring to the boil, then reduce the
heat and simmer for 20-30 minutes until tender. Drain and
set aside.

Leave until cool enough to handle, then peel. Pass the
potatoes through a fine sieve into a bowl while still warm.
Set aside while you prepare the sausage.

Put the sausage in a pan with water to cover over a medium
heat. Bring to the boil, then reduce the heat and simmer for
30-40 minutes until the sausage is cooked.

Drain, reserving 100ml (3½fl oz) of the cooking liquid.
Then cut the sausage into 2cm (¾in) slices.

To complete the aligot, put the butter in a pan over a medium
heat until hot. Add the garlic and cook for 1–2 minutes until
soft but not brown.

Add the cream and milk and bring to the boil. Add the
sieved potatoes and mix thoroughly, then add the grated
Tomme de Laguiole and mix well with a spatula. The aligot
must be very stringy and cheesy. Season with salt, pepper
and nutmeg, then set aside, covered to keep warm.

To complete the sausage, heat a non-stick pan over a medium
heat until hot. Add the sliced sausage and cook for 3–4
minutes to sear all over.

Meanwhile make a mustard sauce by putting the reserved
cooking liquid in a pan with the wholegrain mustard over a
medium heat and stir well.

Just before serving, make sure the aligot is piping hot, or it
will harden. Divide the aligot and sausage between the plates,
drizzle with a little mustard sauce and serve.

PORTOBELLO MUSHROOMS STUFFED WITH WALNUTS AND GORGONZOLA

Preheat the oven to 180°C (350°F/Gas 4).

Then prep your Portobello mushrooms by removing the stalks and placing them, cap side down, on a baking tray. Add 1 tsp butter to each and sprinkle with thyme leaves. Season with salt and pepper, then bake for 10 minutes until slightly soft.

Meanwhile, finely chop the button mushrooms and the stalks from the Portobello mushrooms.

Preheat the grill.

Put 1 tbsp butter in a pan over a medium heat. When it's hot, add the onion and the garlic. Reduce the heat and sweat for 5 minutes until soft but not coloured.

Add the chopped mushrooms, stir and cook for 10 minutes until the mixture is dry. Season with salt and pepper.

Transfer the mixture to a bowl and add half the Gorgonzola, and the parsley, breadcrumbs and walnuts.

Divide the mixture between the Portobello mushroom caps and place under the grill until golden.

Meanwhile, dress the Castelfranco radicchio and celery with the oil and vinegar and season with salt and pepper.

Divide the Portobello mushroom caps and radicchio and celery mixture between the plates. Sprinkle with the remaining Gorgonzola and serve.

SERVES 4

8 large Portobello mushrooms
80g (scant 3oz) unsalted butter
½ tsp thyme leaves
250g (9½oz) button mushrooms
50g (1¾oz) onion, chopped
1 garlic clove, chopped
80g (scant 3oz) Gorgonzola dolce, crumbled
1 tbsp chopped parsley
20g (¾oz) fresh white breadcrumbs
40g (scant 1½oz) walnuts, chopped, plus 8 walnuts, broken, to garnish
1 Castelfranco radicchio, sliced
2 celery sticks, peeled and finely sliced
2 tbsp olive oil
1 tbsp cider vinegar
Salt and freshly ground black pepper

Gorgonzola is made in the Lombardy region of North Italy. It's a blue-veined cheese with a delicate, sweet flavour.

Or look for a lightly veined, soft and creamy cows' cheese with a light piquancy.

RACK OF VENISON WITH SPÄTZLE AND CORNISH BLUE SAUCE

SERVES 2

2 racks of venison
1 sprig of rosemary
2 garlic cloves, crushed
100g (3½oz) unsalted butter
500g (1lb 2oz) cavolo nero,
    tough stems removed
100ml (3½fl oz) double cream
50g (1¾oz) Cornish Blue
125ml (4½fl oz) port (any type)
Salt and freshly ground
    black pepper

For the spätzle
250g (9½oz) plain flour
3 eggs
120ml (4fl oz) water
Pinch of salt
Grating of nutmeg
2 tbsp vegetable oil
50g (1¾oz) unsalted butter
1 tsp chopped chives
1 tsp chopped parsley
Freshly cracked black pepper

Germany's light, droplet-like spätzle dumplings work perfectly with this Cornish Blue sauce. To make spätzle, bring a large pan of salted water to the boil.

Meanwhile, put the flour, eggs, water, salt and nutmeg in a bowl and mix together thoroughly to make a smooth dough. Push the dough through the holes of a colander into the boiling water. As soon as the spätzle rise to the surface of the water, remove with a slotted spoon to a bowl. Toss with the oil and leave to one side while you prepare the venison.

Preheat the oven to 180°C (350°F/Gas 4).

Season the racks of venison all over with salt and pepper. Put a frying pan over a medium heat and when hot, add the venison. Cook, turning occasionally, until coloured all over. Add the rosemary and garlic, then add the butter and reduce the heat. Baste the venison with the foaming butter, then remove to a roasting tin. Roast for 15 minutes for medium meat.

Meanwhile, bring another pan of salted water to the boil. Add the cavolo nero and cook for 4 minutes until tender. Drain then set aside, covered, to keep warm.

For the cheese sauce, put the cream and Cornish Blue in a pan over a low heat and cook, stirring, until the cheese has melted.

To finish the spätzle, put the butter in a pan over a medium heat. When the butter starts to foam, add the spätzle. Toss in the butter until golden and crispy. Add the chives and parsley and season with black pepper.

When the venison is cooked, remove to a plate and leave to rest for few minutes, covered with foil, before carving.

Add the port to the roasting tin, put it over a medium heat and cook, stirring, to deglaze the tin. Strain through a sieve and add to the cheese sauce.

Serve the venison, the spätzle and the cavolo nero with the cheese sauce.

Cornish Blue in made in the county of Cornwall in England. It's a blue-veined cheese with a buttery, mild flavour.

Or look for a young, blue cows' cheese with a gentle character and slight sweetness.

RISOTTO WITH WHITE TRUFFLE AND CASTELMAGNO

To make this risotto a real truffle indulgence, put the uncooked rice and the white truffle in an airtight container for several days. This will allow the fragrance of the truffle to permeate the rice, giving an extra-rich finish.

On the day the risotto is required, put the stock in a pan over a medium heat and bring to the boil. Reduce the heat and keep the stock at a simmer.

Meanwhile, remove the truffle from the rice.

Put 50g (1¾oz) butter in a large pan over a medium heat until hot. Add the shallots and sweat for 5 minutes until soft and translucent, then add the rice.

Stir well to coat the rice with butter. Lightly touch the surface of the rice with your fingertip and when it is hot, add the wine. Stir again and cook for a few minutes until the wine has evaporated.

Pour in the hot stock, a ladleful at a time, so it just covers the rice each time. Wait until each ladleful has been absorbed before adding the next. Keep adding the stock in this way until the rice is just cooked al dente, then remove from the heat. The risotto must not be too dry; if you shake the pan, the rice should be 'wavy' ('all'onda') in the pan.

Set aside for 1 minute. Then add the remaining butter and stir vigorously.

When the butter is well incorporated, add the Castelmagno and season with salt and pepper to taste. You may not need to add salt at all.

Divide between the serving plates and shave the truffle over the top.

SERVES 4

80g (scant 3oz) carnaroli rice
    per person as a starter; 100g
    (3½oz) per person as a main
1 small white truffle
    (approx 40g/scant 1½oz)
2 litres (3½ pints) chicken stock
130g (4½oz) unsalted butter
100g (3½oz) shallots,
    finely chopped
150ml (5fl oz) dry white wine
100g (3½oz) Castelmagno, grated
Salt and white pepper

Castelmagno in made around the Piemont region of North Italy. It's a soft cheese with a grainy, crumbly texture and a tangy flavour which becomes more spicy with age.

Or look for a firm blue cheese made from cows' milk.

STILTON, PEAR AND PORT TERRINE

This terrine needs a day or two in the fridge before it's ready to tuck into, so start at least a day before.

Put the caster sugar and water in a pan over a medium heat. Stir to dissolve the sugar.

Peel the pears, cut in half and remove the cores. Add to the syrup in the pan, reduce the heat and poach for 10 minutes, or until just slightly soft but still crisp. The time required will depend on the type of pear.

Remove from the heat and leave to cool in the syrup. When cold, remove with a slotted spoon and slice thinly.

Next, crumble the Stilton into a bowl with your fingers, then add the port. Mix with your hands until the port is fully incorporated. Do not overwork the mixture.

Line a terrine tin or loaf tin with cling film. Add half the cheese mixture and press down well. Cover any gaps in the cheese with slices of poached pear.

Cover with the remaining cheese mixture and press down again. Refrigerate overnight, or for up to 2 days.

When you're ready to serve, put the walnuts and demerara sugar in a dry pan over a medium heat. Toast until the walnuts are well coated with caramelised sugar. Remove from the heat and crush the walnuts, breaking them up into small pieces.

Unmould the terrine and sprinkle the walnuts over the terrine, making sure they stick to the sides. Slice and serve.

SERVES 10

200g (7oz) caster sugar
500ml (16fl oz) water
1 pear
500g (1lb 2oz) Stilton
60ml (2fl oz) port
(for a more complex, fuller taste, choose a tawny port that has been aged for 10 years in oak; for a younger, sweeter taste, choose a ruby port)
160g (5½oz) walnut halves
1 heaped tbsp demerara sugar
Salt and freshly ground black pepper

Stilton is made in the Midlands in England from cows' milk. It's a blue-veined cheese with a creamy texture and tangy finish which becomes more intense with age.

Or look for a semi-soft blue cheese with a crumbly texture and piquant character.

TARTIFLETTE WITH REBLOCHON

SERVES 4

500g (1lb 2oz) good-quality smoked
    streaky bacon, cut into lardons
2 tbsp vegetable oil
40g (scant 1½oz) unsalted butter
1 onion, finely chopped
2 garlic cloves, finely chopped
1 bay leaf
½ tbsp chopped thyme
4 tbsp plain flour
120ml (4fl oz) dry white wine
600ml (1 pint) double cream
Grating of nutmeg
600g (1lb 5oz) desiree potatoes
200ml (7fl oz) full-fat milk
200ml (7fl oz) water
1 Reblochon
Salt and freshly ground
    black pepper

Reblochon is made in the Savoie
region of South France using
cows' milk. It is rich, fruity and
nutty with a semi-soft, almost
chewy texture.

Or look for a cows' milk cheese
with a washed rind and an earthy
aroma.

This rich potato gratin (designed to show off the mighty
Reblochon) is ever popular with skiers looking for a warming,
filling lunch. It makes an ideal winter dish, whether you're on
the French Alps or not.

Prepare the lardons (cubed bacon) first by putting enough
water to cover them in a large pan over a medium heat. Bring
to the boil. Add the lardons and cook for 10 seconds. This
removes the excess salt. Drain well.

Heat the oil in a pan over a medium heat until hot. Add the
drained lardons and fry for 10–12 minutes until crispy. Remove
with a slotted spoon to kitchen paper to drain.

Next, put the butter in a pan over a medium heat until hot.
Add the onion and garlic and cook for 10 minutes until golden,
then add the bay leaf and thyme. Cook, stirring, for another
couple of minutes, then add the drained lardons and the
flour. Cook for 2 minutes more, then add the wine. Cook for
5 minutes until the wine has evaporated, then add the cream.
Reduce the heat and simmer for 5–10 minutes until the sauce
starts to thicken. Season to taste with salt, if required, and
with pepper and nutmeg. Remove from the heat and discard
the bay leaf.

Preheat the oven to 190°C (375°F/Gas 5).

Peel the potatoes and cut into 5mm (¼in) slices. Rinse under
cold running water, then put in a pan and cover with the milk
and water. Add a few pinches of salt and cook over a medium
heat for 8 minutes until the potatoes are cooked but still
slightly firm. Try not to overcook. Drain well.

Place the potatoes in overlapping rows in an ovenproof dish
and pour the cream and wine sauce on top. Cut the Reblochon
in half widthways, then in half again lengthwise to produce
4 pieces. Place the pieces on top with the rind face up.

Bake in the oven for 10–15 minutes until golden and bubbling.

FRENCH ONION SOUP WITH 18-MONTH-OLD COMTÉ

Is there a dish more synonymous with good, simple French cooking than a rich onion soup? For a really full-bodied bowlful though, you need a strong stock made from chicken bones and vegetables.

To make this, preheat the oven to 190°C (375°F/Gas 5).

Put the chicken bones in a roasting tin and roast in the oven for about 30 minutes until golden brown.

Remove from the oven and put in a large pan with the carrot, celery, onion, 3 bay leaves and the peppercorns. Cover with cold water, bring to the boil, then reduce the heat and simmer for 2 hours. Skim off any impurities that float to the surface.

Meanwhile, make the rest of the soup. Put the oil and butter in a large pan over a medium heat until hot. Add the finely sliced onion. Reduce the heat, season with salt and add the remaining 3 bay leaves. Cook slowly for 20–30 minutes until the onion is golden brown. Do not worry if the onion sticks a little to the pan; this will add to the flavour.

Add the thyme, sprinkle over the flour and cook, stirring, for a few minutes until all the flour is incorporated. Add the wine, increase the heat, and cook for 5 minutes until the wine has evaporated.

Strain the stock through a fine sieve and add to the pan with the onion. Stir well, then reduce the heat and simmer for 1½ hours. Season with salt and pepper.

Preheat the grill.

Divide the soup between 8 flameproof serving bowls, leaving two fingers' depth at the top of the bowl. Add a slice of sourdough bread to each bowl, top with the grated Comté and place under the grill for 5–8 minutes, or until the cheese is golden and bubbling.

SERVES 8

500g (1lb 2oz) chicken bones
1 carrot, cut into chunks
1 celery stick, cut into chunks
1 onion, cut into chunks
6 bay leaves
4 peppercorns
2 tbsp vegetable oil
50g (1¾oz) unsalted butter
1.5kg (3lb 3oz) roscoff onion or
    Spanish onion, very finely sliced
1 tbsp chopped thyme
4 tbsp plain flour
200ml (7fl oz) dry white wine
Salt and freshly ground
    black pepper
350g (12oz) 18-month-old Comté,
    grated, to serve
8 slices of sourdough bread,
    to serve

Comté (18 month) is made in the Franche-Comté region of France using milk from cows which graze only on grass and hay. It has earthy, roasted caramel flavours. Comté is France's most consumed cheese.

Or look for a hard, nutty and buttery cheese.

CHOCOLATE FONDANTS WITH A BLU DI BUFALA HEART

SERVES 5

100ml (3½fl oz) whipping cream
200g (7oz) Blu di Bufala
180g (scant 6½oz) unsalted butter,
 plus extra for greasing
200g (7oz) 70% dark chocolate,
 roughly chopped
6 eggs
200g (7oz) caster sugar
90g (scant 3½oz) plain flour, sieved

Blue cheese and chocolate are natural companions and the Blu di Bufala works brilliantly with the dark chocolate in this crowd-pleasing dessert.

Start by making the gooey centre. Put the cream and 100g (3½oz) Blu di Bufala in a pan over a low heat. Stir until the cheese has melted and the mixture is smooth. Spoon the mixture into an ice cube tray with small compartments and put in the freezer while you prepare the rest of the dish.

Put the butter, chocolate and remaining Blu di Bufala in a heatproof bowl over a bain-marie. Stir until the chocolate has melted and the mixture is smooth.

Whisk the eggs and sugar together in another bowl until well combined. Then add the butter, chocolate and Blu di Bufala mixture. Stir well.

Fold in the flour, then refrigerate for 4–5 hours until the mixture is firm.

Preheat the oven to 190°C (375°F/Gas 5) and butter 5 individual dariole moulds.

Put the mixture in a piping bag fitted with a plain nozzle. Pipe the mixture halfway up each mould. Put a small frozen cube of cream and Blu di Bufala mixture into each mould, then cover with more mixture from the piping bag, leaving a finger's thickness of room at the top of the mould.

Bake 12–15 minutes. Take care not to overcook as the fondants should remain runny in the middle.

Blu di Bufala is made in the Lombardy region of Italy from blue water buffalo's milk. It has a buttery, rich character with tangy blue veins and sweet notes.

Or look for a semi-firm, blue buffalo cheese that's both tangy and sweet.

Very carefully unmould the fondants on to the serving plates and serve immediately.

CORNISH BLUE ICE CREAM WITH CARAMELISED WALNUTS

This cheese ice cream (and the two on the following pages) are endlessly talked-about in the Androuet restaurant – it's a definite hit!

Start by putting the milk, cream, caster sugar, icing sugar, honey and salt in a heatproof bowl over a bain-marie. Warm the mixture gently, stirring occasionally, but do not allow to boil. When the mixture is warm, add the Cornish Blue and stir thoroughly so the cheese melts and the mixture is well combined.

Remove from the heat and leave to cool, then refrigerate for 4 hours. When the mixture is cold, transfer to an ice-cream maker, following the manufacturer's instructions. Halfway through the churning, add the crushed caramelised walnuts. Continue churning until the mixture is well combined.

Serve with each scoop of ice cream decorated with a half-walnut, or transfer to a shallow freezer-proof dish and put in the freezer to eat later.

If you do not have an ice-cream maker, put the chilled mixture in a shallow freezer-proof dish in the freezer. Remove from the freezer every hour, for 3 hours, and whisk with a handheld electric whisk to ensure the ice cream is smooth. Return the ice cream to the freezer one more time until firm.

Remove from the freezer 10 minutes before serving so the ice cream is soft enough to scoop.

MAKES 1 LITRE (1 ¾ PINTS)

600ml (1 pint) full-fat milk
100ml (3½fl oz) whipping cream
200g (7oz) caster sugar
1 tbsp icing sugar
1 tbsp clear honey (such as acacia)
Pinch of sea salt flakes
100g (3½oz) Cornish Blue
10g (¼oz) caramelised walnuts (see Crottin salad and caramelised walnuts, p81), crushed, plus extra caramelised walnut halves, uncrushed, to decorate

Cornish Blue in made in the coastal county of Cornwall in England. It's a blue-veined cheese with a buttery, mild flavour.

Or look for A young, blue, cows' cheese with a gentle character and slight sweetness.

VINTAGE GOUDA ICE CREAM WITH PUMPKIN AND AMARETTI

Preheat the oven to 190°C (375°F/Gas 5).

Peel the pumpkin, cut it into chunks and put on a baking tray. Cover with foil and cook in the oven for 30–40 minutes until soft.

Put the milk, cream, caster sugar, icing sugar, honey, and salt in a heatproof bowl over a bain-marie. Warm the mixture gently, stirring occasionally, but do not allow to boil. When the mixture is warm, add the Gouda and the pumpkin. Stir thoroughly so the cheese melts and the mixture is well combined.

Remove from the heat and leave to cool, then refrigerate for 4 hours. When the mixture is cold, transfer to an ice-cream maker, following the manufacturer's instructions. Halfway through the churning, add the crushed amaretti biscuits. Continue churning until the mixture is well combined.

Serve straight away, or transfer to a shallow freezerproof dish and put in the freezer to eat later.

If you do not have an ice-cream maker, put the chilled mixture in a shallow freezerproof dish in the freezer. Remove from the freezer every hour, for 3 hours, and whisk with a handheld electric whisk to ensure the ice cream is smooth. Return it to the freezer one more time until firm.

Remove from the freezer 10 minutes before serving so the ice cream is soft enough to scoop.

MAKES 1 LITRE (1 ¾ PINTS)

100g (3½oz) pumpkin
600ml (1 pint) full-fat milk
100ml (3½fl oz) whipping cream
220g (scant 8oz) caster sugar
1 tbsp icing sugar
1 tbsp clear honey (such as acacia)
Pinch of sea-salt flakes
70g (2oz) vintage Gouda
2 tbsp crushed amaretti biscuits

Gouda is made in Holland using cows' milk. Its character changes considerably as it ages. Aged Gouda is hard with flavours of dried fruits and toasted seeds.

Or look for a mature Gouda or a rich, hard cows' milk cheese.

GOATS' CHEESE ICE CREAM WITH THYME AND HONEY

It's important to find the freshest goats' cheese you can before making this ice cream – it's the key to the perfect scoop.

Put the milk, cream, caster sugar, icing sugar, salt and 1 tbsp honey in a heatproof bowl over a bain-marie. Warm the mixture gently, stirring occasionally, but do not allow to boil. When the mixture is warm, remove from the heat and leave to cool to room temperature.

Add the goats' cheese and stir thoroughly to combine, then blend until smooth with a handheld blender.

Refrigerate for 4 hours. When the mixture is cold, transfer to an ice-cream maker, following the manufacturer's instructions. Halfway through the churning, add the thyme and remaining honey. Continue churning until the mixture is well combined.

Serve straight away, or transfer to a shallow freezerproof dish and put in the freezer to eat later.

If you do not have an ice-cream maker, put the chilled mixture in a shallow freezerproof dish in the freezer. Remove from the freezer every hour, for 3 hours, and whisk with a handheld electric whisk to ensure the ice cream is smooth. Return it to the freezer one more time until firm.

Remove from the freezer 10 minutes before serving so the ice cream is soft enough to scoop.

MAKES 1 LITRE (1 ¾ PINTS)

580ml (20fl oz) full-fat milk
90ml (3fl oz) whipping cream
200g (7oz) caster sugar
1 tbsp icing sugar
2 tbsp clear honey (such as acacia)
Pinch of sea-salt flakes
200g (7oz) fresh goats' cheese, grated
1 heaped tsp finely chopped thyme

ANDROUET FONDUE

SERVES 2

180ml (6½fl oz) dry white wine
2 tbsp cornflour
340g (12oz) 18-month-old Comté, grated
60g (2oz) Emmental Grand Cru, grated
1 garlic clove
Black peppercorns

To serve
Selection of charcuterie
Cornichons
1 crispy baguette, cut into cubes

A good fondue requires the best cheese you can buy – at Androuet, we use 18-month old Comté and Emmental Grand Cru for a thick, golden fondue that's hard to forget. You can use other cheeses, but it's best to discuss the most suitable cheeses with your cheesemonger before embarking on your own special blend of fondue.

To start, put the wine and cornflour in a pan over a medium heat. Whisk well until the mixture starts to thicken, then add the grated Comté and Emmental. Reduce the heat and stir over a low heat with a spatula until the cheese has melted and is bubbling.

Meanwhile, heat a cast-iron fondue dish. When it's hot, crush the garlic in it, then add the bubbling cheese. Sprinkle with freshly cracked black pepper and serve immediately with the charcuterie, cornichons and cubed baguette.

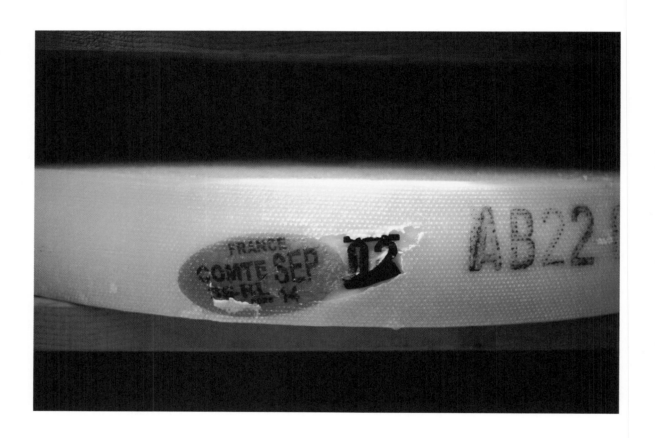

WINTER
CHEESEBOARD

Perl Las

A delicate blue-veined cheese dubbed the 'blue pearl' by its Welsh producers

Mont d'Or Vacherin

A soft cows' cheese from Jura that's rich, creamy and slightly sweet (see p137)

Tomme de Montagne

A semi-hard cows' cheese from Savoy, made in the French mountains (see p125)

Comté 32 months

A Comté from Jura aged longer for more intense earthy, nutty and roasted caramel flavours

Langres

From the Champagne-Ardenne region of France, this soft cows' cheese is very festive and is ideal served with a glass of champagne

SERVING THE PERFECT CHEESEBOARD

Preparing a good cheeseboard is all about balance. Firstly it looks most attractive when there are an odd number of cheeses on the board: three, five or seven. Secondly, try to have a soft, a hard and a blue cheese; then to try to have different types of milk – cow, sheep and goat. You need to think about balancing the taste and texture of the various cheeses.

For quantity, we recommend thinking about total grams per person, then dividing that by the number of cheeses on the board. If you're planning a cheeseboard at the end of a meal, you'll need about 80g (3oz) per person. For a cheese dinner served with some charcuterie and nibbles, it's about 120g (4.5oz). Then for a cheese-only dinner, it's about 200g (7oz) per person. So if you want 120g per person and three cheeses, allow 40g of each cheese per person.

To store cheese, keep it in its original packaging in the vegetable box of your fridge (the drawer in the bottom) and take it out 30 minutes before serving.

The best fruits to serve with a cheeseboard are pears or grapes, because their acidity cuts through the natural creaminess of the cheese. If neither are in season, just select an acidic fruit.

In France, we generally serve baguette with cheese. In the UK and US, crackers tend to be preferred. In France, for some people it's wrong to eat butter with cheese, for others it's a must (it really depends on where you're from). We think that you should go with what makes you happy, and that goes for the cheese on the board too. So if you don't like blue cheese (for example), just leave it off and add more of your favourite. That's the only way to enjoy it.

Bonne dégustation!

COMPLEMENTARY WINES

When selecting our wine for the shop and restaurant, we follow the same approach that we do for our cheese – always put taste first. But equally important to us is knowing the producers and having an affinity with their production style and methods.

As a result, most of the wines we stock have a few things in common: they have a balanced taste, the vineyards they come from use minimal (or no) pesticides and the producers tend to be small (the largest estate we stock is only around 20 hectares).

The producers we work with generally define themselves more as gardeners than winemakers, and they believe once the grapes are harvested there should be as little human intervention as possible. We believe that if vines are carefully taken care of, then the grapes will taste great and so will the wine.

Vineyards that don't use pesticides have to use natural techniques to fight plant sicknesses. An example is recreating an ecosystem in the vineyard which will naturally cure any diseases: this is what's known as a biodynamic technique. Some of the most prestigious winemakers are now converting (or already use) this technique, such as Château Palmer in Bordeaux and Domaine de la Romanée-Conti in Burgundy.

An open mind is the key to discovering great wine. We sometimes find people drink certain wines for their labels or for where they come from instead of for their taste. So for this book we've decided to recommend styles of wine, rather than wine regions or vineyards. This will make your wine purchasing (from an independent seller, of course) a whole lot easier...

- With fresh cheese (such as Mozzarella and Brillat-Savarin), go for sparkling white wines.

- With fresh goats' cheese (such as Chabichou), go for a dry and minerally white wine.

- With soft cheese with a bloomy rind (such as Brie and Camembert), go for red wines with subtle tannins.

- With mature goats' cheese (such as Sainte Maure de Touraine), go for a light and fruity red.

- With blue cheese (such as Bleu d'Auvergne or Stilton), go for dessert wines or fortified red wines.

- With semi-hard cheese (such as St Nectaire and Morbier), go for light- to medium-bodied red wines.

- With mountain hard cheese (such as Comté or Gruyère), go for oxidised white wines from Jura, or pair with a sherry.

- With cheddar-style hard cheese (such as Montgomery or Laguiole), go for crisp white wines or light/medium red wines.

- With washed rind cheese (such as Epoisses or Petit Livarot), go for red wine with low tannins.

- Finally, with a cheeseboard, go for white wines over reds because the tannins in red wines accentuate the saltiness of the cheeses.

That being said, we strongly believe there are no rules! Just have fun and drink your favourite wines with your favourite cheeses.

Santé!

INDEX

A

Aarewasser 128, 131
aligot 145
almonds: almond crumble 63
    bourdaloue tart with whipped Petit Suisse 126
Alpine cheeses 67
Androuet 23, 25
Androuet, Henri 25
Androuet, Pierre 25
Androuet fondue 167
artichokes: globe artichokes with
        Délice des Cabasses 39
    paimpol bean and baby artichoke stew 89
asparagus: asparagus with rolled Rove des
        Garrigues 32
    green and white asparagus with Red Leicester
        crisps 72
aubergines: aubergine caviar 49–50
    aubergine, confit tomato and St Tola terrine 70
    pickled aubergine 76

B

bacon: tartiflette with Reblochon 155
Barkham Blue 98
basil oil 79
bavettes au Roquefort 105
beans: paimpol bean and baby artichoke stew 89
Beaufort 131
Beaufort d'Alpage 20
Beaufort d'Eté 98
beef: bavettes au Roquefort 105
    beef cheeks with Gruyère Etivaz and
        horseradish mash 138
beer: Montgomery Cheddar and pale ale rarebit 109
beetroot, goats' curd and pine kernel salad 55
Berkswell 89
    pork fillet in a Berkswell crust 89
blancmange 63
Bleu d'Auvergne 178
Bleu des Causses 142
    duck breast with sarladaise potatoes and

Bleu des Causses turnip tops 141–2
Bleu du Val d'Aillons 128
Blu di Bufala 159
    chocolate fondants with a Blu di Bufala heart 159
blue cheeses 67
    Bleu des Causses 142
    Blu di Bufala 159
    Cornish Blue 149, 160
    Gorgonzola 146
    Roquefort 105
    Stilton 152
    wines to accompany 178
bourdaloue tart with whipped Petit Suisse 126
bread: Einkorn, Westcombe Cheddar and confit
        onion bread 112
    grilled vegetable tartine with tapenade and Fleur
        du Maquis 43
    lamb navarin with Souréliette-topped toast 46
    Montgomery Cheddar and pale ale rarebit 109
    Raclette and Emmental croque-monsieur 110
Brie 178
    Emmental, Brie and Serrano ham croquettes 106
Brillat-Savarin 29, 35, 60, 128, 178
    Brillat-Savarin cheesecake with marinated
        cherries 60
    smoked duck breast with baby gem, Brillat-Savarin
        and mixed berries 35
Brousse 52, 58
    'cigars' with Brousse 58
    pasta rolls with Brousse and sundried tomatoes 52
Buffalo Mozzarella with pickled aubergine and
        red pepper coulis 76
butternut squash: roast butternut squash with
    vintage Gouda 122

C

Camembert 64, 134, 178
    baked Camembert with rosemary, honey and
        almonds 134
caramel: caramelised walnuts 81, 160
cardamom and Lincolnshire Poacher crisps 117

Castelmagno 150
    risotto with white truffle and Castelmagno 150
cauliflower, Montgomery Cheddar and pale
    ale rarebit 109
celeriac: potato, celeriac and parsnip mash 121
Chabichou 29, 178
Chabichou du Poitou 57
    Chabichou du Poitou röstis with girolles and
        poached duck eggs 57
Chalet Alpage 20
champagne: blancmange, rhubarb and champagne
    and almond crumble 63
Cheddar 101
    Einkorn, Westcombe Cheddar and confit onion
        bread 112
    Montgomery Cheddar and pale ale rarebit 109
cheeseboards 175
cheesecake, Brillat-Savarin 60
cherries, marinated 60
chicken: poulet de Bresse with potato, celeriac and
        parsnip mash and Morbier sauce 121
chocolate fondants with a Blu di Bufala heart 159
chorizo: baby spinach, chorizo and Manchego salad 75
'cigars' with Brousse 58
Clacbitou 36
    Clacbitou soufflés with a pea coulis 36
clafoutis with peaches and La Tur 94
Comté 18, 131, 156, 167, 170, 178
    Androuet fondue 167
    French onion soup with 18-month-old Comté 156
Cornish Blue 149, 160
    Cornish Blue ice cream 160
    rack of venison with spätzle and Cornish Blue
        sauce 149
courgette flowers, Ricotta-stuffed 40
cows' cheese: Brillat-Savarin 29, 35, 60, 128, 178
    Camembert 64, 134, 178
    Castelmagno 150
    Comté 18, 131, 156, 170, 178
    Emmental 106, 110
    Fourme d'Ambert 85

Gouda 122, 162
Gruyère 114
Gruyère Etivaz 138
La Tur 94
Lincolnshire Poacher 117
Mont d'Or 131, 137, 170
Montgomery Cheddar 109
Morbier 121, 178
Ogleshield 87
Pave d'Auge 64
Ossau-Iraty 29, 40
Raclette 110
Reblochon 155
Red Leicester 72
Roquefort 105
Tomme de Laguiole 145, 178
Tomme de Montagne 125
West Country Farmhouse Cheddar 101
Westcombe Cheddar 112
cream: blancmange 63
crisps: Parmesan, cardamom and Lincolnshire
        Poacher crisps 117
    Red Leicester crisps 72
croque-monsieur, Raclette and Emmental 110
croquettes: Emmental, Brie and Serrano ham 106
Crottin de Chavignol 81
    Crottin de Chavignol salad with caramelised
        walnuts 81
crudités, Fourme d'Ambert dip with 85
crumble, almond 63
cucumber: tzatziki 49–50
curd cheeses: Délice des Cabasses 39, 98
    Feta 82
    Petit Suisse 126
custard, rum 96

D
Délice des Cabasses 29, 39, 98
    globe artichokes with Délice des Cabasses 39
dip, Fourme d'Ambert 85
dressing, ewes' yogurt 93

INDEX

duck: duck breast with sarladaise potatoes and
     Bleu des Causses turnip tops 141–2
  smoked duck breast with baby gem, Brillat-Savarin
     and mixed berries 35
duck eggs: Chabichou du Poitou röstis with girolles
     and poached duck eggs 57

E
eggs: asparagus with rolled Rove des Garrigues
     and soft-boiled eggs 32
  baby spinach, chorizo and Manchego salad with
     soft-boiled eggs 75
  Chabichou du Poitou röstis with girolles and
     poached duck eggs 57
Einkorn, Westcombe Cheddar and confit onion
     bread 112
Emmental 106
  Androuet fondue 167
  Emmental, Brie and Serrano ham croquettes 106
  Raclette and Emmental croque-monsieur 110
Epoisses 178
ewes' yogurt 93
  tuna Niçoise with a ewes' yogurt dressing 93

F
Feta 82
  Feta and watermelon salad 82
fig and Ricotta tart 96
fishcakes, haddock and Ogleshield 87
Fleur du Maquis 43
  grilled vegetable tartine with tapenade and Fleur
     du Maquis 43
fondue, Androuet 167
Fort des Rousses 18
Fourme d'Ambert 64, 67, 85
  Fourme d'Ambert dip with crudités 85
fregola with Ossau-Iraty and Ricotta-stuffed
     courgette flowers 40
French onion soup with 18-month-old Comté 156
fresh cheeses: homemade fresh cheese 44
  wines to accompany 178

fromage blanc 63
  blancmange 63
fruit, cheeseboards 175

G
galettes Bretonnes with wild mushrooms
     and Gruyère 114
girolle mushrooms, Chabichou du Poitou
     röstis with 57
globe artichokes with Délice des Cabasses 39
goats' cheeses 101
  Chabichou 29, 57, 178
  Crottin de Chavignol 81
  goats' cheese ice cream with thyme and honey 164
  La Tur 94
  Rove des Garrigues 32
  St Nicolas de la Dalmerie 90
  St Tola 70
  wines to accompany 178
goats' curd 55
  roast beetroot, goats' curd and pine kernel salad 55
goats' milk yogurt 50
  tzatziki 49–50
Gorgonzola 146
  Portobello mushrooms stuffed with walnuts and
     Gorgonzola 146
Gouda 122, 162
  roast butternut squash with vintage Gouda 122
  vintage Gouda ice cream with pumpkin and
     amaretti 162
Grano, Alessandro 27
green and white asparagus with Red Leicester
     crisps 72
Gruyère 114, 178
  beef cheeks with Gruyère Etivaz 138
  galettes Bretonnes with wild mushrooms
     and Gruyère 114
Gruyère Etivaz 138
Guarneri, Alex 23
Guarneri, Laurence 23
Guarneri, Léo 23

H

haddock and Ogleshield fishcakes 87
ham: Emmental, Brie and Serrano ham croquettes 106
    Raclette and Emmental croque-monsieur 110
hard cheeses, wines to accompany 178
Herault 67
horseradish mash 138

I

ice cream: Cornish Blue ice cream 160
    goats' cheese ice cream with thyme and honey 164
    vintage Gouda ice cream with pumpkin and
        amaretti 162

K

kale: pork belly with sweet potato mash, rainbow
    kale and aged Pecorino Sardo 118

L

La Tur 94
    clafoutis with peaches and La Tur 94
Laguiole see Tomme de Laguiole
lamb: lamb navarin with Souréliette-topped toast 46
    spiced lamb rump with aubergine caviar quenelles,
        tomato confit and yogurt tzatziki 49–50
Langres 170
Leicester see Red Leicester
Lincolnshire Poacher 101, 117
    Lincolnshire Poacher crisps 117
Lou Sounal 98

M

Manchego 75
    baby spinach, chorizo and Manchego salad 75
mayonnaise, truffle 57
Mont d'Or 131, 137, 170
    Mont d'Or melt 137
Montgomery Cheddar 109, 178
Morbier 121, 178
    poulet de Bresse with potato, celeriac and parsnip
        mash and Morbier sauce 121

morels: veal paupiettes with morels and Tomme
    de Montagne 125
Morteau sausage with aligot 145
Mozzarella, Buffalo 76, 178
    Buffalo Mozzarella with pickled aubergine and
        red pepper coulis 76
mushrooms: Chabichou du Poitou röstis with
        girolles and poached duck eggs 57
    galettes Bretonnes with wild mushrooms and
        Gruyère 114
    Portobello mushrooms stuffed with walnuts and
        Gorgonzola 146
    veal paupiettes with morels and Tomme de
        Montagne 125

O

Ogleshield 87
    haddock and Ogleshield fishcakes 87
oil, basil 79
olives: tapenade 43
onions: Einkorn, Westcombe Cheddar and confit onion
        bread 112
    French onion soup with 18-month-old Comté 156
Ossau-Iraty 29, 40
    fregola with Ossau-Iraty and Ricotta-stuffed
        courgette flowers 40

P

paimpol bean and baby artichoke stew 89
pale ale: Montgomery Cheddar and pale ale rarebit 109
pancakes: galettes Bretonnes with wild mushrooms
        and Gruyère 114
Parmesan crisps 117
parsnips: potato, celeriac and parsnip mash 121
pasta: fregola with Ossau-Iraty and Ricotta-stuffed
        courgette flowers 40
    pasta rolls with Brousse and sundried tomatoes 52
pastries: 'cigars' with Brousse 58
Pave d'Auge 64
peaches: clafoutis with peaches and La Tur 94
peas: Clacbitou soufflés with a pea coulis 36

INDEX

Pecorino Sardo 118
    pork belly with sweet potato mash, rainbow kale
        and aged Pecorino Sardo 118
peppers: red pepper coulis 76
Perl Las 170
Petit Livarot 178
Petit Suisse 126
    bourdaloue tart with whipped Petit Suisse 126
pickled aubergine 76
pork: pork belly with sweet potato mash, rainbow kale
        and aged Pecorino Sardo 118
    pork fillet in a Berkswell crust with a paimpol bean
        and baby artichoke stew 89
port: Stilton and port terrine 152
Portobello mushrooms stuffed with walnuts and
        Gorgonzola 146
potatoes: aligot 145
    Chabichou du Poitou röstis 57
    haddock and Ogleshield fishcakes 87
    horseradish mash 138
    Mont d'Or melt 137
    potato, celeriac and parsnip mash 121
    sarladaise potatoes 141–2
    sweet potato mash 118
    tartiflette with Reblochon 155
poulet de Bresse with potato, celeriac and parsnip
        mash and Morbier sauce 121
pumpkin: vintage Gouda ice cream with pumpkin
        and amaretti 162

R
Raclette 110
    Raclette and Emmental croque-monsieur 110
rarebit, Montgomery Cheddar and pale ale 109
Reblochon 155
    tartiflette with Reblochon 155
Red Leicester 72
    Red Leicester crisps 72
rhubarb: blancmange, rhubarb and champagne
        and almond crumble 63
rice: risotto with white truffle and Castelmagno 150

Ricotta 79, 96
    chilled tomato soup with Ricotta 79
    fig and Ricotta tart 96
    Ricotta-stuffed courgette flowers 40
risotto with white truffle and Castelmagno 150
Roquefort 105
    bavettes au Roquefort 105
röstis, Chabichou du Poitou 57
Rove des Garrigues 32, 64
    asparagus with rolled Rove des Garrigues 32
rum custard 96

S
Sainte Maure de Touraine 178
St Nectaire 178
St Nicolas de la Dalmerie 67, 90
    tomato tarte tatin with St Nicolas de la Dalmerie 90
St Tola 70
    aubergine, confit tomato and St Tola terrine 70
salads: baby spinach, chorizo and Manchego salad 75
    Crottin de Chavignol salad 81
    Feta and watermelon salad 82
    roast beetroot, goats' curd and pine kernel salad 55
    roast butternut squash with vintage Gouda 122
    tuna Niçoise with a ewes' yogurt dressing 93
Salers 128
samphire: globe artichokes with Délice des
        Cabasses 39
sarladaise potatoes 141–2
sauce vierge 72
sausages: Morteau sausage with aligot 145
semi-hard cheeses, wines to accompany 178
Serrano ham: Emmental, Brie and Serrano ham
        croquettes 106
sheeps' milk cheese: Berkswell 89
    Brousse 52, 58
    La Tur 94
    Lou Sounal 98
    Manchego 75
    Pecorino Sardo 118
    Ricotta 40, 79, 96

Souréliette 46, 98
sheep's yogurt see ewes' yogurt
shrimps: brown shrimp sauce 87
smoked duck breast with baby gem, Brillat-Savarin
    and mixed berries 35
soft cheeses 101
    Fleur du Maquis 43
    wines to accompany 178
soufflés, Clacbitou 36
Soumaintrain 128
soups: chilled tomato soup with Ricotta and
        basil oil 79
    French onion soup with 18-month-old Comté 156
Souréliette 46, 98
    lamb navarin with Souréliette-topped toast 46
spätzle 149
spinach: baby spinach, chorizo and Manchego salad 75
squash: roast butternut squash with vintage
        Gouda 122
Stilton 131, 152, 178
    Stilton and port terrine 152
sweet potato mash 118

T
tapenade 43
tartiflette with Reblochon 155
tarts: bourdaloue tart with whipped Petit Suisse 126
    fig and Ricotta tart 96
    tomato tarte tatin with St Nicolas de la Dalmerie 90
terrines: aubergine, confit tomato and St Tola
        terrine 70
    Stilton and port terrine 152
tomatoes: aubergine, confit tomato and St Tola
        terrine 70
    chilled tomato soup with Ricotta and basil oil 79
    pasta rolls with Brousse and sundried tomatoes 52
    sauce vierge 72
    tomato confit 49–50
    tomato tarte tatin with St Nicolas de la Dalmerie 90
Tomme 29, 101
Tomme de Laguiole 145, 178

Morteau sausage with aligot 145
Tomme de Montagne 125, 170
    veal paupiettes with morels and Tomme de
        Montagne 125
truffles: risotto with white truffle and
        Castelmagno 150
    truffle mayonnaise 57
tuna Niçoise with a ewes' yogurt dressing 93
turnip tops, Bleu des Causses 141–2
tzatziki 49–50

V
Vacherin Fribourgeois 131
veal paupiettes with morels and Tomme de
        Montagne 125
vegetables: Fourme d'Ambert dip with crudités 85
    grilled vegetable tartine with tapenade and
        Fleur du Maquis 43
    see also peppers, tomatoes etc
venison: rack of venison with spätzle and Cornish
        Blue sauce 149

W
walnuts: caramelised walnuts 81
    Cornish Blue ice cream with caramelised
        walnuts 160
    Portobello mushrooms stuffed with walnuts
        and Gorgonzola 146
    Stilton and port terrine 152
washed rind cheeses, wines to accompany 178
watermelon: Feta and watermelon salad 82
West Country Farmhouse Cheddar 101
Westcombe Cheddar 64, 112
wines 177–8
    Androuet fondue 167
    beef cheeks with Gruyère Etivaz 138
    rhubarb and champagne 63

Y
yogurt: tuna Niçoise with a ewes' yogurt dressing 93
    tzatziki 49–50

ACKNOWLEDGEMENTS

We would like to thank the many friends and colleagues we are lucky enough to have in our lives…

To Monsieur Stéphane Blohorn, owner of Androuet in Paris, for his trust and support in carrying on the Androuet name and heritage in London.

To chef Alessandro Grano for his dedication and friendship, and for creating beautiful recipes. When we first met, we didn't know that we'd become like brothers and we're grateful for your hard work.

To our parents and family for their love and support.

To our commissioning editor Zena Alkayat for her patience, hard work and faith in the project from the start.

To photographer Kim Lightbody who was game enough to travel around France with Alex as her guide, and for her artistic take on Androuet and our recipes.

To all the people we've worked with and collaborated with over the years, including our cheesemongers, service staff and producers – this book is also yours.

To the chefs and restaurant managers who have understood our approach to cheese so beautifully and have allowed us to build a reputation we are proud of.

And finally, to our customers. We are honoured to have such loyal customers with whom we've formed a close relationship over the years. We look forward to bringing you more delicious cheese to discover.

Right: A red seal is only applied to Souréliette when the producers are satisfied it is of the highest quality. Overleaf: French goats' cheese Selles-sur-Cher and Gruyère Etivaz